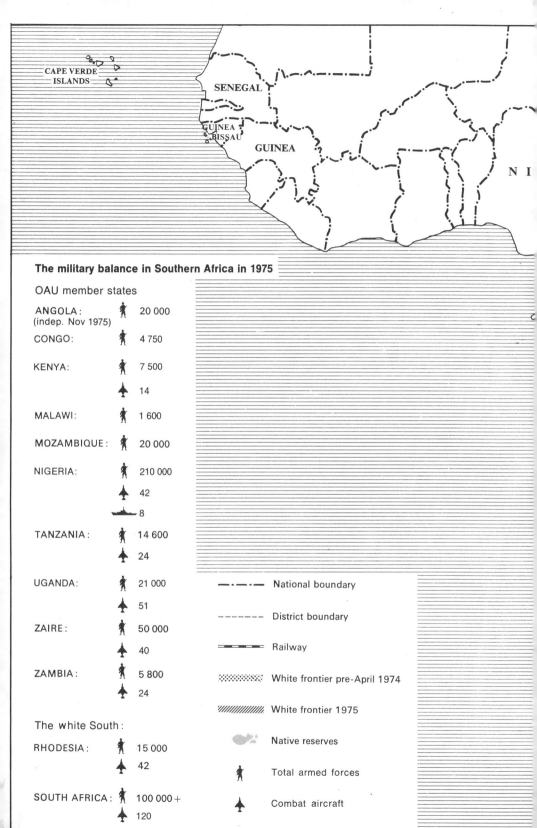

CAPE VERDE
ISLANDS

SENEGAL

GUINEA-
BISSAU

GUINEA

N I

The military balance in Southern Africa in 1975

OAU member states

ANGOLA: 👤 20 000
(indep. Nov 1975)

CONGO: 👤 4 750

KENYA: 👤 7 500
                 ✈ 14

MALAWI: 👤 1 600

MOZAMBIQUE: 👤 20 000

NIGERIA: 👤 210 000
                 ✈ 42
                 🚢 8

TANZANIA: 👤 14 600
                 ✈ 24

UGANDA: 👤 21 000
                 ✈ 51

ZAIRE: 👤 50 000
                 ✈ 40

ZAMBIA: 👤 5 800
                 ✈ 24

The white South:

RHODESIA: 👤 15 000
                 ✈ 42

SOUTH AFRICA: 👤 100 000 +
                 ✈ 120
                 🚢 30

—·—·— National boundary

------- District boundary

═══════ Railway

▓▓▓▓▓ White frontier pre-April 1974

▨▨▨▨▨ White frontier 1975

🐟 Native reserves

👤 Total armed forces

✈ Combat aircraft

🚢 Heavy warship

LiberKartor Stockholm 1976

Horse Injuries
their Prevention and Treatment

Horse Injuries
their Prevention and Treatment

Roberta Baxter

The Crowood Press

First published in 1999 by
The Crowood Press Ltd
Ramsey, Marlborough
Wiltshire SN8 2HR

www.crowood.com

This impression 2002

British Library Cataloguing in Publication Data

A catalogue record for this book is available from the British Library.

ISBN 1 86126 260 4

Dedication
For Potter, and my other four-limbed friends.

Black and white photographs by the author, except the one on page 149,
which is by Stuart Baxter.
Line-drawings by Elizabeth Mallard-Shaw

Edited and designed by OutHouse Publishing Services
Printed in Great Britain by The Bath Press, Bath

Contents

Acknowledgements—

Without the help and support of my colleagues at the Old Golfhouse Veterinary Group, and our clients this book would not have been possible. I should also like to thank Jo Baxter, Roz Cole and David Walmsley for their invaluable assistance in proof-reading the manuscript, and Adam for his patience.

Introduction ———————————

As both a horse owner and a veterinary surgeon I can appreciate the difficulties associated with the assessment and management of injured horses. The initial assessment of equine injuries is of pivotal importance to the outcome of any situation, and this is usually carried out by the horse owner.

This book has four main aims. The first is to assist the owner in the assessment of both common and uncommon equine injuries. The second is to aid the decision-making process as to when to call in a vet. The third is to help the owner identify whether an injury can successfully be managed without veterinary assistance. The fourth is to explain the processes that occur during injury and in the onset of diseases related to such injuries.

The first chapters deal with the preventative measures that can be taken in order to avoid injuries, and give an overview of the principles of first aid and the assessment of emergency situations. The middle section of the book is divided into chapters according to the area of the body that is affected, with an extra chapter covering injuries that can present as acute collapse – always an emergency. Chapters are further divided into subsections, each describing a particular type of injury and how it may prevent itself, and outlining the types of treatment available, and the likely outcome. Finally, an appendix helps to explain the aims of the main types of medication used in the horse, and a glossary of technical terms is included to assist your understanding of vetspeak!

Whilst this book aims to be a useful guide to identifying and treating injuries, it must be reiterated that if you aren't sure what to do, always call a vet – even if it is for no other purpose than to discuss the situation.

1 Preventing Injuries

Preventative medicine should be the cornerstone of good horse care. Attention to the management of your horse from the standpoint of preventing injuries and disease, and promoting health can result in a happier and healthier horse that performs

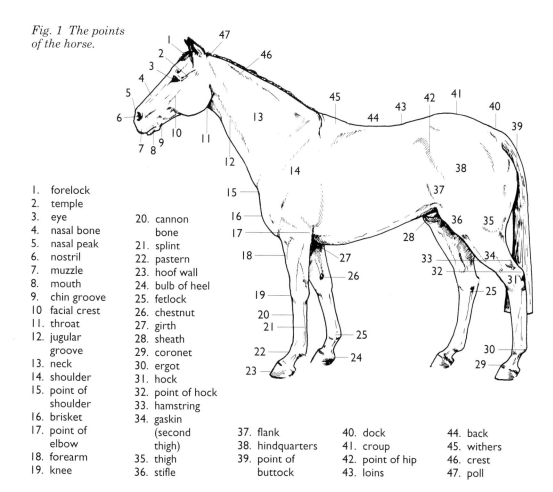

Fig. 1 The points of the horse.

1. forelock
2. temple
3. eye
4. nasal bone
5. nasal peak
6. nostril
7. muzzle
8. mouth
9. chin groove
10 facial crest
11. throat
12. jugular groove
13. neck
14. shoulder
15. point of shoulder
16. brisket
17. point of elbow
18. forearm
19. knee
20. cannon bone
21. splint
22. pastern
23. hoof wall
24. bulb of heel
25. fetlock
26. chestnut
27. girth
28. sheath
29. coronet
30. ergot
31. hock
32. point of hock
33. hamstring
34. gaskin (second thigh)
35. thigh
36. stifle
37. flank
38. hindquarters
39. point of buttock
40. dock
41. croup
42. point of hip
43. loins
44. back
45. withers
46. crest
47. poll

1. occipital bone
2. zygomatic arch
3. orbit (eye socket)
4. malar bone
5. nasal bone
6. incisors
7. molars
8. mandible
9. scapula (shoulder blade)
10. first rib
11. humerus
12. sternum
13. olecranon (point of elbow)
14. radius
15. ulna
16. carpus (knee joint)
17. accessory carpal bone
18. metacarpus
19. splint (small metacarpal)
20. cannon (great metacarpal)
21. proximal sesamoid
22. 1st phalanx (P1)
23. 2nd phalanx (P2)
24. 3rd phalanx (P3)
25. navicular bone
26. ribs
27. costal cartilage
28. metatarsus
29. cannon (great metatarsal)
30. splint (small metatarsal)
31. tarsus (hock joint)
32. talus
33. calcaneus
34. tibia
35. fibula
36. stifle joint
37. patella
38. femur
39. great trochanter
40. ischium
41. ilium
42. tuber coxa
43. tuber sacrale
44. coccygeal vertebrae
45. sacral vertebrae
46. lumbar vertebrae
47. thoracic vertebrae
48. cervical vertebrae
49. axis
50. atlas

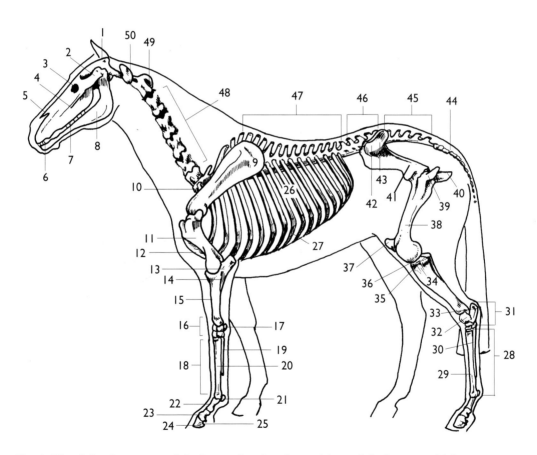

Fig. 2 The skeletal anatomy of the horse, showing the positions of the bones and joints.

1. brachiocephalicus
2. splenius
3. rhomboideus
4. serratus ventralis
5. cranial deep pectoral
6. trapezius
7. latissimus dorsi
8. gluteal fascia
9. superficial gluteal
10. semitendinosus
11. coccygeus
12. tensor fasciae latae
13. fasciae latae
14. biceps femoris
15. soleus
16. long digital extensor
17. lateral digital extensor

18. deep digital flexor
19. gastrocnemius
20. tibialis caudalis
21. tibialis cranial
22. external abdominal oblique
23 external intercostal
24. serratus ventralis
25. pectoralis
26. flexor carpi ulnaris
27. flexor carpi radialis
28. lateral digital extensor
29. ulnaris lateralis
30. common digital extensor
31. extensor carpi radialis
32. brachialis
33. triceps
34. deltoideus

35. supraspinatus
36. subclavius
37. sternocephalicus
38. masseter
39. zygomaticus
40. labia inferior
41. obicularis oris
42. caninus
43. levator nasolabialis
44. obicularis oculi
45. corrugator supercilli
46. parotido auricularis

A common extensor tendon
B lateral extensor tendon
C suspensory ligament
D deep digital flexor tendon

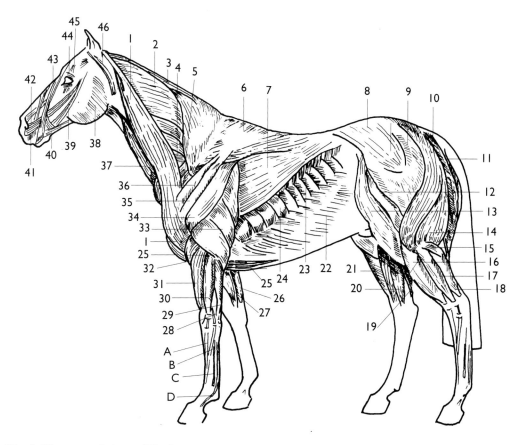

Fig. 3 The musculature of the horse.

at the highest possible level with reduced need for veterinary attention. This in turn can lead to a happier and richer owner!

Preventative medicine starts with choosing and buying the right horse, and continues with managing him in ways that help to avoid injury. The insurance of horses is also to be advised so that when injuries do occur the course of action taken can be dictated by most the most appropriate treatment for the horse, rather than the cost.

When choosing a horse, the first thing to consider is the specific purpose you have in mind for him. Even if he is wanted only for light hacking, it is still important that he has no major health problems and is of a suitable age, size and strength to carry the rider. If you wish to use the horse in competiton, your requirements will be more specific, and you will need to pay closer attention to his conformation.

CONFORMATION

When choosing a horse, or indeed when considering whether to use one for breeding, it is worth bearing in mind that certain aspects of conformation can predispose a horse to the occurrence of certain types of injury. Horses with ideal conformation are rare, but assessment of conformation is important so that the likelihood of future injuries can be assessed.

The Head and Neck

Horses with particularly large heads tend to work predominantly on their forehands, and this can cause neck and shoulder muscle strain as well as an increased likelihood of forelimb disease. The set of the neck is important too, because it

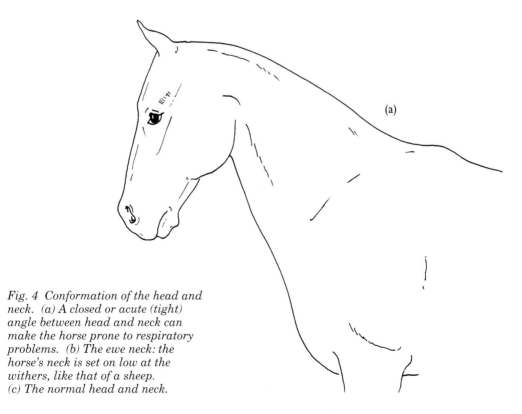

(a)

Fig. 4 Conformation of the head and neck. (a) A closed or acute (tight) angle between head and neck can make the horse prone to respiratory problems. (b) The ewe neck: the horse's neck is set on low at the withers, like that of a sheep. (c) The normal head and neck.

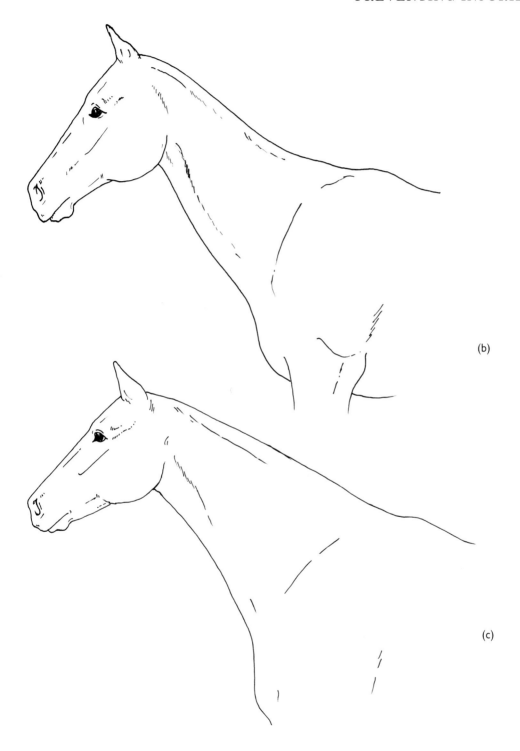

(b)

(c)

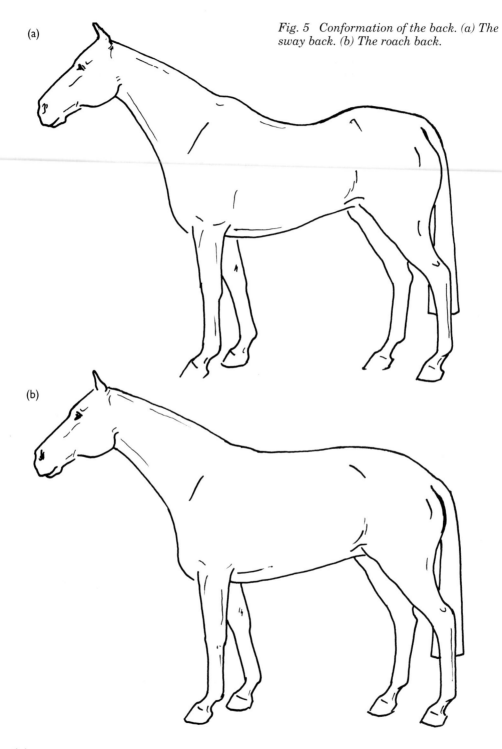

(a)

(b)

Fig. 5 Conformation of the back. (a) The sway back. (b) The roach back.

relates to the position and alignment of the larynx. If the angle of the head on the neck is too acute (*see* Fig. 4a), there is an increased chance of laryngeal problems occurring. The shape of the neck affects the horse's ability to flex and accept the bit: horses with 'ewe' necks (*see* Fig. 4b) may therefore be more difficult to control, and more prone to back problems.

The Back

The shape of the back can relate to both the strength of the back, and that of the hind limbs. The back that is too long is more likely to become injured than a shorter one, but short backs have an increased chance of vertebral problems because the likelihood of adjacent spinous processes impinging upon one another ('kissing spines') is increased. 'Sway' and 'roach' backs (*see* Fig. 5) are to be avoided because of the increased incidence of problems associated with such conformation.

From the side, the profile of the ideal horse should fit a square (*see* Fig. 6): the height of the horse at the withers and the rump should equal his length from brisket to hindquarters.

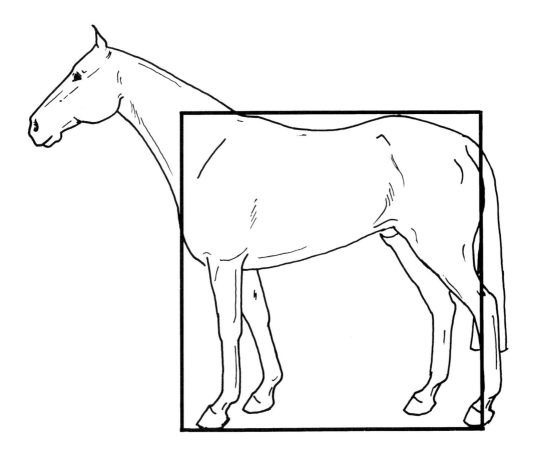

Fig. 6   The profile of the horse's body should fit into a square.

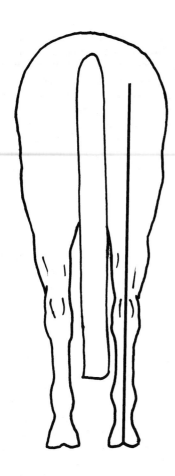

Fig. 7 The set and alignment of the hind limb (viewed from the back). A plumb-line dropped from the point of the hip should bisect the limb. Note the muscle symmetry on the rump as well as the limb and foot symmetry.

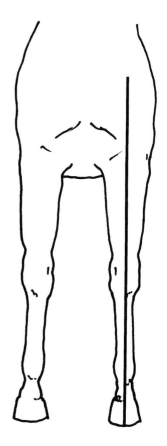

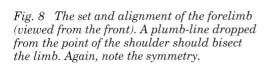

Fig. 8 The set and alignment of the forelimb (viewed from the front). A plumb-line dropped from the point of the shoulder should bisect the limb. Again, note the symmetry.

The Limbs

Probably the two most important aspects of conformation are the set of the limbs (which includes the breadth of the chest) and the straightness of the limbs' alignment. The weight of the horse is transmitted directly through his limbs: the weight of the horse's head means that 60 per cent of the bodyweight is borne by the forelimbs, and only 40 per cent by the hind limbs, which are used more for propulsion.

Horses are designed so that their weight should normally be borne symmetrically through the middle of all the main joints of the limbs; however, any deformity of the limbs can cause the weight to be borne asymmetrically through the joints, and this can result in abnormal stresses and thus an increased chance of injury. The higher in the limb the source of a deviation, the greater the likelihood that problems will result. Further discussion of how and why conformational abnormalities can cause lameness is to be found in Chapter 11.

In the ideal horse, the bone and muscle structure of the limbs are symmetrical when viewed from behind or in front. From the back of the horse, a plumb-line dropped from the point of the buttock down the back of the hind limb should bisect all the joints, to end at the centre of the hoof (see Fig. 7). When viewing the horse from in front, a plumb-line dropped from the point of the shoulder to the ground should pass down the centre of the limb to the mid-point of the foot (see Fig. 8).

When the horse is viewed from the side, a plumb-line dropped on the outside of the forelimb from the spine down the middle of the shoulder blade should pass down the centre of the limb, bisecting the joints, and reach the ground at the centre of the foot. Similarly, a plumb-line dropped from the point of the hip on the hind limb should bisect the hoof. The fore and hind legs should be well put together. Horses that are 'back at the knee' may sustain increased stress to their flexor tendons; and horses that are 'over at the knee' or 'straight hocked' may have shortened or contracted flexor tendons.

When the horse moves, the limbs should move freely and equally, and should swing straight, rather than plaiting, brushing, or dishing.

The Feet

Ideally, each foot should be symmetrical from side to side (see Fig. 9a), and the fore and hind feet should be two matching pairs. If, for instance, one foot is more upright and 'boxy' than the other it may indicate that a problem is likely.

When viewed from the side, the midpoint of the coffin joint (one-third of the way back along the coronary band) should lie directly above the middle of the weight-bearing surface of the foot (see Fig. 9b). The slope of the toe should match that of the pastern. In the forelimb, the angle between the toe and the sole should be approximately 45–50 degrees; in the hind limb, which is slightly more upright, this angle is increased to 50–55 degrees.

The bulbs of the heels should be elevated from the ground, but the heels of the hoof should be weight-bearing and should not be contracted. The sole should be arched and firm and should not be in contact with the ground; the frog should be firm and elastic. Viewed from below the foot should appear symmetrical, and the distance from one heel to the toe should equal the width of the foot (see Fig. 9c).

Where the conformation of the feet deviates from this, abnormal stresses may be passed through the limbs and so increase the chances of various types of lameness occurring.

17

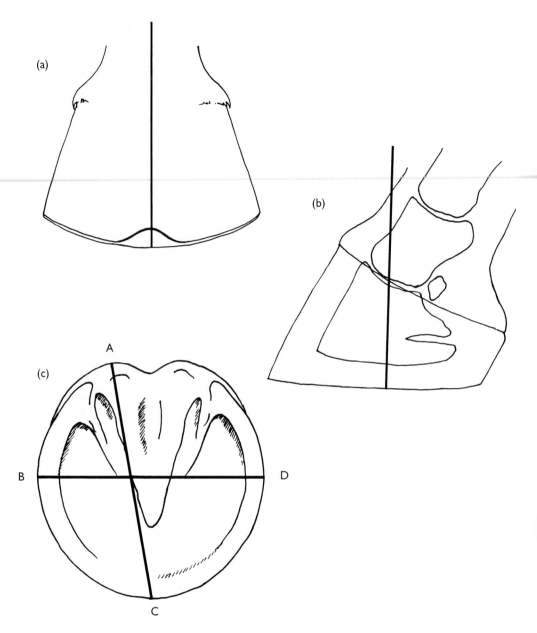

Fig. 9 Conformation of the foot. (a) From the front, the foot should be symmetrical about a line dropped through the centre of the limb. The line should be perpendicular to the weight-bearing surface of the foot. (b) From the side, a line dropped from a point a third of the way along the coronary band (which overlies the mid-point of the coffin joint) should bisect the weight-bearing surface of the foot. (c) From below, the foot should be symmetrical, and the distance from one heel to the toe (A to C) should be the same as the width of the foot (B to D).

VETTING

Vetting, or pre-purchase examination, of a horse by a vet is always a good idea. This involves a full examination of the horse and will include an approximate estimation of his age, which aids assessment of whether or not he is capable of the work for which he is intended.

Even if the price of the horse is little more than the cost of the vetting, it is still advisable to have it carried out because it can be devastating, either financially or emotionally – or both – to discover that a horse has a condition that pre-existed your purchase and prevents you from being able to enjoy him.

The Vetting Procedure

The standard 'vetting' procedure consists of five stages and involves thorough examination of the horse for any signs of unsoundness, such as lameness, and any symptoms of disease. A vetting certificate, which is provided on completion of the examination, attests to the soundness of the horse on that day, when subjected to the specified procedure. What it does not do is give any kind of guarantee of whether or not the horse has, or will develop, any diseases that are currently causing no symptoms. Nor does it certify the absence of vices or the reproductive status of the individual.

Blood Sampling

It is often a good idea to obtain a blood sample at the time of the vetting and have it checked for painkillers. Permission for this procedure has, by law, to be given by the vendor. A guarantee can then be obtained to the effect that should the horse subsequently become lame, and analysis of the blood show the presence at the time of the vetting of non-steroidal anti-inflammatory drugs (painkillers such as bute), the vendor will refund the money. The purchaser can thus be given protection against disreputable vendors who would otherwise sell horses that have known lameness problems but that appear sound as a result of the recent administration of medication.

Vice Warranties

A warranty regarding lack of vices may also be obtained from the vendor. This is a matter between the vendor and the purchaser, but it is not uncommon for purchasers to request a written warranty to say that the horse suffers from no vices, such as crib-biting or windsucking, that can predispose him to injury or disease. The vendor agrees to refund the purchase price if the horse then exhibits these vices within an agreed period of time after the sale.

Other information that the purchaser should question the vendor about includes what the horse is like to shoe, to clip and to box, and how he is in traffic, and with the vet!

Reproductive Status

The reproductive status of the horse is not part of an official vetting procedure, but pregnancy can be certified where appropriate and, where necessary, semen analysis can be carried out.

The Pre-purchase Examination

The vetting procedure consists of a five-stage process, although this may be reduced at the request of the purchaser of a young, unbroken, or unfit horse.

Stage 1

This is the preliminary stage, which consists of a complete clinical examination, including examination of the teeth to gain an approximate idea of the age of the horse. Attention is paid to all the horse's systems, which include the muscles, bones and joints, the skin, the heart and lungs, and the eyes.

Stage 2

This entails trotting the horse over 20–40 yards (18–36m) on firm, level ground. Soundness is assessed, and the procedure is halted at this stage if the horse is lame.

Stage 3

This consists of a period of strenuous exercise, which is usually carried out under the saddle, and should involve a five- to ten-minute canter, with the horse passing the vet on each circuit so the vet can assess respiratory noise as well as look for signs of lameness. A controlled gallop should also be included. Immediately after this exercise the heart and lungs are checked again.

Stage 4

This consists of half an hour's rest, during which further examination can be carried out, and the horse's markings can be recorded.

Stage 5

This is a final trot-up, during which the horse is once again assessed for soundness. Flexion tests are also carried out by most vets at this time. Although their usefulness is sometimes disputed, most vets agree that if flexion tests are assessed carefully they can help to determine whether there is likely to be underlying joint disease. If the vet and/or the purchaser are concerned about any of the joints, X-rays can be taken. X-rays are not taken routinely, however, since slight abnormalities can sometimes be seen in horses that are, and remain, clinically normal.

VICES

Common vices include crib-biting, windsucking, weaving, and head-shaking; less commonly, self-mutilation may also be seen. All of these vices can be associated with injuries, health problems, or an inability to perform, and in many cases these behaviours are related to boredom or stress. Often horses learn them from other affected horses that share their environment.

Whatever the vice, treatment is more effective the earlier it is carried out. It should be centred around making the horse's environment more interesting so that boredom is reduced and the horse is distracted from such behaviour. Feeding stabled horses their hay from nets with small holes – so that it takes them longer to eat it – can help to keep them occupied. Toys are worth considering as many horses enjoy playing with horseballs and other toys whether in the stable or in the field. Turning affected horses out for as much time as possible can also be helpful, although some horses will just stand by the gate and crib, rather than bothering to graze. The judicious use of electric fences may help to prevent this.

Crib-biting and Windsucking

Both crib-biting and windsucking can contribute to digestive disorders, and thus may be implicated in cases of colic. Some horses can be prevented from these types of behaviour by removing objects that they can crib-bite or by painting them with a proprietary bitter-tasting material. Using a cribbing strap can also be helpful, but some horses are able to crib or wind-suck in any situation, and may even incorporate these vices into head-shaking.

Weaving

Weaving can pre-dispose a horse to concussion-related injuries of the limbs, can result in poor weight gain, and can prevent horses from box-resting effectively where this is necessary. Many horses continue to weave even if weaving grills are put up.

Self-mutilation

Self-mutilation is extremely rare, but is most often seen in stallions that are kept in alone for much of the time. They may begin to chew their flanks or stifles, which can cause open wounds. In some cases horses that have sustained injuries may obsessively remove dressings and attempt to mutilate affected areas. The fitting of a cradle to prevent them from reaching such areas can be helpful.

GENERAL MANAGEMENT

Turn-out

Fencing should be checked regularly, and any sharp objects such as nails, wire, or sharp stones should be dealt with promptly. Post-and-rail fences are preferable because they are stronger, do not involve wire which can so easily cause cuts, and are easily visible, so horses are less likely to collide with them. Where wire fences must be used, barbed wire should never be present; and where possible, a wooden upper rail should be added. Shelter or rugging should be available in bad weather, stables and shelters should be adequately bedded, suitable food should be provided, and water should always be available.

Horses should be turned out in the same group where possible. Horses are creatures of habit and are happiest if they are always turned out with their usual companions. This makes them more likely to settle down and graze rather than to gallop around and possibly injure themselves. When a new horse is to be introduced to a group, it is usually best to lead him out to graze in hand for a while before turning him loose. It is usually advisable to avoid turning out mares and geldings together, since seasonal behaviour of mares can easily lead to conflict and kicks.

Feeding

A suitable type and amount of nutrition should be provided for your horse's needs. Most horses have a forage-based diet with grass or hay providing the bulk of their requirements. Hard feed is usually provided to supplement the protein and energy content in the diet of working or pregnant horses. If you are unsure of the most appropriate way to feed your horse, and the quantity and type of hard feed needed, seek the advice of an equine nutritionist. Most of the main feed companies employ such staff who can advise you.

Overfeeding a pony (and thus running the risk of his getting laminitis) is as much of a problem as expecting a horse to compete on a less than adequate diet. When gauging the appropriate weight for a horse, a useful measure is that the ribs should be palpable, but not visible (although the ribs are always visible in some very fine Thoroughbreds and full-ribbed Arabians).

Fields should be continually monitored for the presence of poisonous plants. The most significant of these are Ragwort, Yew and acorns. Other plants that can cause problems include Bryony, Bog Asphodel, Nightshade, Bracken, Privet, and a variety of other wildflowers and garden plants, including Laburnum, Rhododendron, Foxgloves, St John's Wort, poppies, various bulbs, and even buttercups. Ragwort is usually avoided by horses unless they have nothing else to eat; but in its dried form it becomes more palatable, so if it is incorporated into hay the horse may then eat large amounts of it. Ragwort causes liver damage, which can be fatal. Yew is extremely poisonous, being toxic to the heart. Only a very small amount can rapidly cause death. Acorns are extremely palatable to most horses, and can cause kidney damage and diarrhoea.

Horses that are prone to sand colic, or that graze fields where sand colic is likely (because the ground is dry and the grass is short and sparse), may be fed Isogel (psilium), which aids the passage and expellation of ingested sand and so helps to prevent the condition. Isogel can be mixed into food regularly once weekly as a preventative measure. To ascertain whether or not sand is present in a horse's dung, the droppings should be mixed thoroughly with water in a bucket, the contents allowed to settle, and the water and dung then gently poured off. If present, sand and earth will settle at the bottom of the bucket.

Fig. 10 Horses are happiest when turned out in familiar groups.

Oak Yew Common Ragwort

Creeping
Buttercup

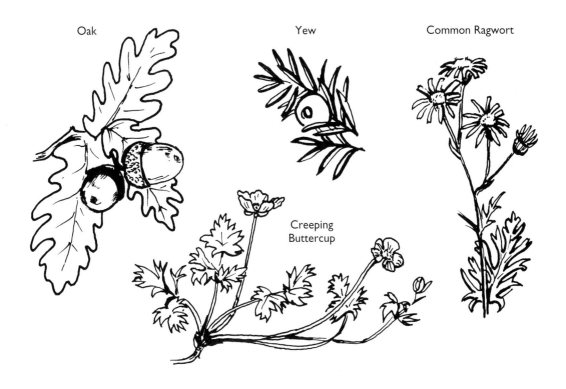

Fig. 11 Some of the plants that are poisonous to horses.

Where a special diet is required for medical reasons it should be followed; giving a horse with COPD (chronic obstructive pulmonary disease) poor-quality, unsoaked hay is bound to result in problems. In fact giving any animal poor hay increases the risk of his developing COPD. It is also worth bearing in mind that the horse is designed to be a foraging animal, and whilst continual stabling and lack of grazing may not cause digestive problems it does increase the likelihood of dental problems developing. The horse is designed to prehend (take in) grass with his incisors, and to chew it with his molars. Horses that do not graze do not wear down their incisors as fast as their molars, and this can cause difficulties.

DENTISTRY

If a horse cannot chew his food properly he cannot digest it properly, and many horses have dental problems of some sort. Teeth should be checked regularly by your vet. In most cases a once-yearly examination at the time of vaccination is sufficient, but in teenage and older horses twice-yearly checks may be necessary.

Sharp teeth can cause injury to the tongue and the insides of the cheeks. Often, the rasping of the outside of the upper molars (*see* Figs 12 and 35) and the inside of the lower molars to remove sharp edges is all that is required. However, many horses do develop more serious tooth irregularities as they get older,

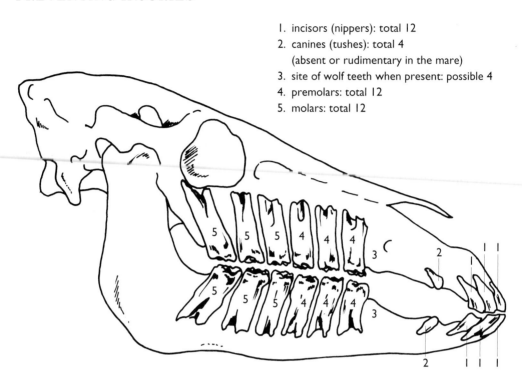

1. incisors (nippers): total 12
2. canines (tushes): total 4
   (absent or rudimentary in the mare)
3. site of wolf teeth when present: possible 4
4. premolars: total 12
5. molars: total 12

Fig. 12   The position and significance of the teeth.

and the removal of hooks, the trimming of overgrown teeth, and even tooth removal may be indicated. Removal of wolf teeth in young horses is also often necessary.

Poor dental treatment can cause serious injuries, such as fractured jaws. In the UK, the current legal position is that removal of teeth must be carried out by a veterinary surgeon. There are some very competent and well-qualified equine dentists, but others are poorly equipped and lacking in knowledge. If you wish to use an equine dentist, ask your vet to recommend one.

WORMING

The importance of regular worming can't be overemphasized in a discussion of the prevention of injury and disease. All horses are continuously exposed to a variety of species of worm. Some types are well tolerated and cause few or no ill effects, even when they are present in large numbers. But some can – even in small numbers – cause serious internal injuries and disease.

Common signs of worm infestation include ill thrift, poor coat, pot belly, colic (up to 70 per cent of some types of colic are worm-related), weight loss, diarrhoea, and, in some cases, liver disease.

No single worming treatment kills all the different types of parasite, and so a carefully planned regime, using a range of drugs to target different species of worm at appropriate times in their life-cycles is necessary.

The life-cycles of worms are typically divided between time spent developing into infective agents on the pasture or in the environment, and time spent within the horse. Certain measures, such as collecting the dung twice weekly, can be used to reduce the numbers of infective parasites on the pasture. This helps to avoid build-up of worms, and increases the amount of available grazing. It is also wise to avoid overgrazing fields as excess grazing increases the likelihood that a horse will ingest worm eggs. Reseeding pastures from time to time, as well as resting or rotating the available grazing yearly between horses and sheep or cattle, helps to reduce parasite numbers.

Anti-helminthics (or wormers) are used to kill parasites or to promote their passage from horses to reduce infestation. Within the 24 to 48 hours after worming, the horse's body will expel live worms, which are then able to reinfect horses (*see* Fig. 13). It is therefore important to treat all horses on the same pasture at the same time (missing even just one horse on the

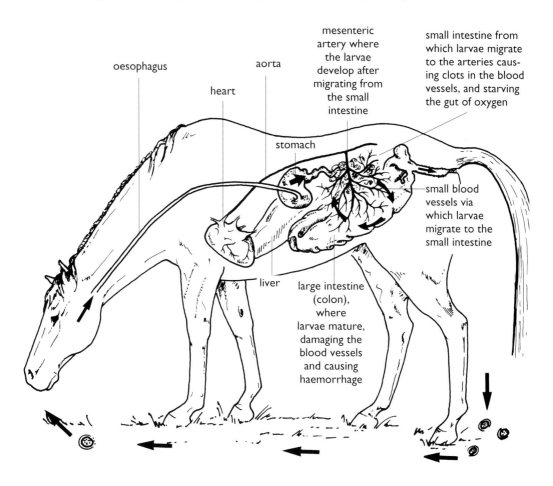

Fig. 13 The life-cycle of the large strongyle (redworm).

25

premises puts all the other horses at risk from worm-related disease), and also to stable horses or move them on to fresh pasture for one to two days after worming. New horses entering a yard should be isolated, stabled immediately and wormed with a broad-spectrum wormer.

Horses are wormed according to their bodyweight, so it is important to give each horse the right dose for his size to ensure his treatment is effective. As a rough guide, the average well-built Thoroughbred-type horse weighs around 1,210–1325lb (550–600kg), whilst a lightly built 13.2hh. pony might weigh approximately 770lb (350kg).

The formula for calculating a horse's approximate weight is as follows:

$$\text{Weight (kg)} = \frac{\text{girth (cm}^2) \times \text{length (cm)}}{11,900}$$

(length = point of shoulder to point of buttocks [ischium] – see Fig. 2)

Significant Parasites

Large Strongyles

Large strongyles are extremely pathogenic, and cause the most problems whilst in the migratory phase of their life-cycle. Eggs from the pasture hatch into larvae, and when these are ingested by the horse they burrow through the gut wall into the arterial system. After further development, they are carried back to the guts where they develop into adults and lay eggs which are passed in the dung.

Whilst in the arterial system the larvae can damage the organs they pass through, such as the liver, which can cause fatal blockages or rupture of the arteries. Damage to the vessels supplying the guts can also cause loss of oxygen supply and subsequent death of sections of bowel. This causes the symptoms of severe colic and necessitates surgery if the horse is to be saved.

Small Strongyles

Small strongyles (or cyathostomes) can also cause serious diseases. Their life-cycle is similar to that of the large strongyles, but the larvae stay in the gut wall while they develop and therefore cause no damage to the arterial system. The larvae do, however, damage the gut wall, and adult worms can affect gut motility. Diarrhoea and severe colic can result, particularly in the springtime when the larvae emerge together from the gut wall to become adults.

Tapeworms

Large numbers of tapeworms can cause problems when they cluster around the junction between the small and large intestine. Gut ulceration and inflammation can result as well as alterations in gut motility and, in some cases, blockage and even rupture.

Roundworms

Roundworms rarely cause problems in adult horses because most horses over two years of age have well-developed immunity to them. Foals, however, are very susceptible.

When eggs develop in the gut the resultant larvae migrate through the liver and lungs, causing damage on their way. On returning to the gut the larvae develop into adults in such large numbers that blockage of the gut, and subsequent rupture, can occur. In some cases abnormal bowel motility results in the telescoping of the gut and development of an intussusception, which may require surgery. Low-grade colic, weight loss and ill thrift can also be seen.

26

A sensible worming regime	
Late winter/early spring	Five-day course of Panacur Guard.
Early spring	Double dose of Pyratape P/ Strongid P.
Late spring to early autumn	Every four to ten weeks depending on the type used.
	Year 1 – Eqvalan/Furexel/Panomec/Equest. Year 2 – Pyratape P/Strongid P. Year 3 – Panacur/Telmin.
Mid-autumn	Double dose of Pyratape P/ Strongid P
Latte autumn	Five-day course of Panacur Guard.
Early winter	Eqvalan/Furexel/Panomec/Equest.

Bots

Bots are not worms, but the larval stages of the bot fly, which lays its eggs on the horse's hair. The eggs cause irritation, which induces the horse to groom himself with his lips and tongue and so ingest them. In the stomach they hatch into larvae and attach themselves to the stomach wall, where they continue to develop, causing inflammation and, in some cases, ulceration. The matured larvae are then passed in the horse's dung, where they develop into adult flies.

Pinworms

Pinworms develop within the horse's bowel, but are relatively innocuous. The females migrate to the skin around the anus and tail base to lay their eggs, and can cause marked irritation in this area.

Stomach Worms

Stomach worms can cause inflammation in the stomach. Infection occurs when larvae are carried to skin wounds by flies, and then migrate through the body to the stomach.

A Practical Worming Regime

The treatment of parasites is necessarily complex. No wormer treats all worms, and so a regime that incorporates the use of different antiparasitic drugs at the times when the worms are vulnerable in the body is needed.

At any particular establishment, the resident worm population can develop resistance to a group of anti-parasitic drugs where these have been overused. This most commonly occurs with the benzimidazole group of drugs. When this happens, the effect of these drugs is reduced, and an alternative regime must be used. Although in most yards these drugs continue to be efficacious, the possibility of worm resistance should be considered if horses show signs of worm-related disease despite regular treatment. If necessary, your vet can examine horse dung for the presence of worm eggs before and after treatment to investigate the efficacy of wormers used.

During the grazing season all horses should be wormed every four to ten weeks. The type of wormer should be rotated year by year (and not dose by dose) to help avoid

27

the development of resistance in worms. The three classes of drug which can be used in this rotation are the benzimidazoles (e.g. Panacur, Telmin), pyrantel (e.g. Pyratape P/Strongid P), and the ivermectins (e.g. Eqvalan/Furexel/Panomec/Equest). Pyrantel should be used every four to six weeks, the benzimidazoles may be used every six to eight weeks, and the ivermectins need only be used every eight to ten weeks.

It is therefore important not only to worm your horse regularly, but to use the right drug at the right time, and to ensure that all horses kept together undergo the same routine at the same time. In addition to worming during the summer, tapeworms are treated with a double dose of pyrantel in early spring and early autumn. It is also worth giving a dose of an ivermectin, or a five-day high-dose course of a benzimidazole, in early and late winter to try to kill the larval stages of the small and large strongyles. Bots can be treated in early winter with a dose of a drug containing ivermectin.

Following the suggested regime (see box, page 27) gives the best possible control of internal parasites and the problems associated with their infestation. However, even with such a regime, horses can have worm-related problems and internal injuries; and if such disease is suspected, a dung sample should be submitted to your vet for analysis.

VACCINATION

The importance of vaccination against tetanus (see Chapter 8) cannot be overemphasized. This disease does kill horses, and treatment is both prohibitively costly and rarely successful. A primary course of two injections is given four to six weeks apart, and a booster is required every two to three years. Vaccination provides some protection against tetanus when minor wounds occur, but tetanus can occur despite vaccination following contamination of wounds. When wounds are seen, therefore, veterinary attention should be sought because a dose of ready-made tetanus antitoxin may be required. Newborn foals should also be given a dose of tetanus antitoxin to protect them until their vaccination course can begin at three to five months of age. In addition, it is a good idea to give pregnant mares their yearly booster approximately four to six weeks prior to their expected foaling date to maximize the immunity passed on to the newborn foal.

Vaccination against flu is also advisable. Although rarely a killer, this disease is costly and frustrating to treat and can easily result in missed competitions. It is fortunate that the vaccination is a requirement for most events. The primary course consists of two injections given approximately four to six weeks apart (depending on the individual brand of vaccine), a further booster needs to be given after six months, and then yearly boosters are required. In order to comply with the UK's Jockey Club rules, which are the requirements of most shows, rides and Pony Club events, the interval between the two primary vaccinations must be between 21 and 92 days, and the third injection should be given between 150 and 215 days after the second one. Horses may compete as soon as they have had both of the primary injections and ten days have elapsed since the second of these.

Vaccination against herpes virus (a common cause of coughs, which can also cause more serious symptoms, including high temperatures, collapse, nervous diseases and abortion), is also possible, and is being increasingly carried out. Other vaccinations may be necessary in breeding animals. Your vet will be able to advise you on the most appropriate vaccination regime for your horse.

The yearly vaccination appointment is an ideal time for discussing with your vet any minor problems that are concerning you. At the same time, it is worth asking your vet to examine your horse for signs of any problems, and to check your horse's heart so that its function can be monitored.

FOOTCARE

Good foot care is extremely important. The feet should be picked out at least once daily. This helps to avoid solar punctures, and to allow rapid recognition of those that occur. In addition, regular foot care should prevent thrush, a bacterial infection of the frog which can only occur in an oxygen-free environment such as that that exists in a poorly cleaned foot.

The slightest imbalance in the hoof can cause abnormal strains in the joints and predispose the horse to lameness problems (*see* Chapter 11). Feet should be trimmed and shod (where necessary) by a competent farrier who should ensure that the hooves are properly balanced and of equal length. This sounds obvious but it is not uncommon to see uneven feet; some feet do not grow symmetrically. For this reason regular farriery every five to six weeks is necessary. Even if a horse's hooves do not appear to be particularly overgrown after this time, they may well be causing abnormal stresses higher in the limb.

Shoeing of the feet should provide evenly distributed support to the whole foot. It is common to see shoes applied to the toes, which do not reach the heels, particularly on the long-toed, low-heeled Thoroughbred type of horse. Instead the shoe should be applied in such a way that it provides support to the heels, and, if they are contracted, helps to encourage them to spread back.

Conformational abnormalities may be improved by appropriate farriery if this is started in the foal or young horse. Corrective shoeing may not necessarily lead to normal appearance of severely affected limbs, but may still help to normalize the stresses within such limbs.

Although specialized surgical farriery may be necessary in animals with laminitis, navicular syndrome, sheared heels, sensitive soles, corns, and a variety of other causes of lameness, good farriery may help to prevent the development of such conditions.

EXERCISE

Exercise levels should be appropriate for the horse's capabilities and fitness. Fitness is not merely a matter of whether or not a horse becomes breathless. Adaptation of the bones and soft tissues, to enable them to cope better with the stresses present, occurs during an ascending regime of exercise. Horses that are not sufficiently fit for the work they attempt are more likely to become injured. This is because stress adaptation will not have

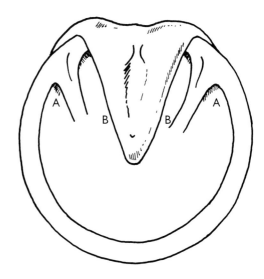

Fig. 14 Seat of corn (A); area affected by thrush (B).

taken place, and so the limbs may be unable to withstand the stresses of such exercise. In addition, tired and unfit horses are more likely to misplace a foot, trip, fall, or crash into a jump, than horses who are fit and fresh.

Arthritic horses respond best to small amounts of regular exercise, and may well be able to cope with light hacks as long as these are regular, and hard ground is avoided. Horses with arthritis may be more likely to trip, particularly if they are trying to move at speed, since their ability to flex up the lower joints of the limbs may be reduced. Horses with other types of concussion-related disease (see Chapter 11) should avoid hard work and, in particular, jumping on hard ground.

TACK

Tack should be examined at the time of its purchase by someone with experience in tack-fitting, and it should thereafter be checked regularly to ensure it fits well and does not rub. As horses gain or lose weight or muscle, they may change in shape and require new tack, or restuffing of existing saddles. Similarly, a horse that has previously suffered injuries in the saddle area may need his saddle restuffed, especially if he does not have symmetrical musculature. Back injuries caused by poor saddle fit, or the use of a damaged or poorly stuffed saddle, are extremely common.

Suitable boots and bandages should be worn, where necessary, for exercise. Overreach boots can help to prevent overreach injuries. Brushing boots can help to prevent brushing injuries, but there is no evidence that they help to protect the tendons against tendon strains.

TRAVELLING

For travelling, good upkeep of trailers and boxes is obviously important as damaged partitions or bars can easily injure horses. Partitions and walls should be padded. The floor should be of suitable material, and be bedded so as to avoid its becoming slippery and so increasing the chance that the horse may slip or fall. Suitable travelling attire, such as travelling boots and light rugs, is also useful in most cases.

INSURANCE

A pre-emptive approach to healthcare should also include insurance for vet's fees. It is easy to run up a huge bill for conditions such as severe lameness and colic that require operations. Insurance enables your horse to have whatever treatment is necessary.

Before you have your horse insured do ask other horse owners for their advice on which insurance company to use; you may find some companies are able to avoid paying out on claims by recourse to the small print on policies.

2 Examining Your Horse

Preventative medicine relies on avoiding problems by recognizing their potential causes, and taking appropriate action promptly; it therefore includes ensuring the safe management of horses in order to reduce the likelihood of injuries occurring.

The recognition of early signs of disease is extremely important in helping to avoid exacerbating problems when they occur. Horses should be examined daily for cuts, grazes and any other signs of illness. Each horse is an individual, so to appreciate signs of ill health you must examine your horse when he is well so that you are familiar with his normal characteristics.

THE VITAL SIGNS

A basic clinical examination that can be done by the owner includes measuring the temperature, pulse and respiration rates of the horse, assessing the colour of the mucous membranes (e.g. the gums), checking for dehydration, and listening for gut noise. This type of examination can assist the horse owner when deciding whether or not to call a vet, and the information it provides can in any case by helpful to the vet when he arrives.

Temperature

The normal temperature of a horse is 99.8–100.5°F (37.6–38°C). Horses in unremitting pain often show slight increases in temperature as a direct consequence of the pain; the other commonest reason for an increased temperature is a severe infection. Temperatures that are mildly elevated need not necessarily be cause for concern, but anything over 101.5°F (38.6°C) is usually significant, and temperatures in the region of 103–105°F (39.4–40.5°C) indicate a very serious problem.

The temperature can be measured with a normal thermometer (if using a mercury thermometer make sure the level of mercury is shaken down before use to avoid incorrect readings). The thermometer should be inserted 1½ inches (4cm) into the rectum (*see* Fig. 15), and held there for about a minute before removing it and reading the result. It is important to insert it towards the side of the rectal canal to avoid measuring the temperature of any dung within the rectum rather than that of the horse himself. After use, mercury thermometers should be shaken down again to avoid incorrect readings in the future. All thermometers should then be cleaned with antiseptic.

Heart Rate and Pulse

The normal resting heart rate (or pulse rate) of a horse is 25 to 40 beats per minute. Foals have a higher heart rate than this, and horses that are extremely fit and very relaxed can have a lower heart

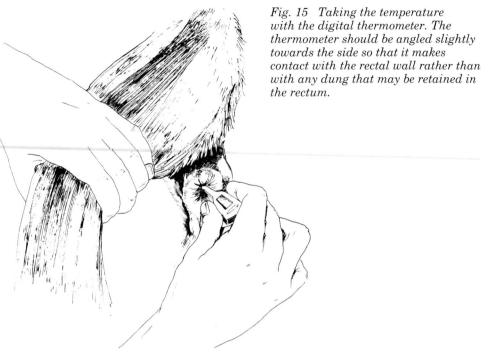

Fig. 15   Taking the temperature with the digital thermometer. The thermometer should be angled slightly towards the side so that it makes contact with the rectal wall rather than with any dung that may be retained in the rectum.

rate. After exercise the heart rate is often elevated to 60 beats per minute, or even higher. In fit horses this heart rate drops to normal within 20 or 30 minutes of cessation of exercise, but in horses that are less fit the heart rate can remain elevated for longer. Horses in unremitting pain or distress (such as those with fractured bones or severe colic) often have elevated heart rates that may be sustained in the region of 60 to 100 beats per minute.

The heart rate can be measured directly in most horses by placing the hand just underneath the elbow on the left-hand side of the chest. The pulse rate can be measured by placing the ball of a finger over one of the arteries and measuring the number of pulsations per minute. The easiest place to find an artery to do this is at the point where the facial artery crosses the angle of the jaw (*see* Fig. 16): if you run your fingers gently but firmly along the angle of the jaw, you will feel a soft tube with dimensions similar to that of an electric flex crossing the jawbone. If the balls of the fingers are placed on this structure, and a slight amount of pressure is applied, pulsation can be felt. You should also be able to find the pulse in the transverse facial artery, which runs in a groove of bone above the eye, and the carotid artery in the neck (*see* Fig. 16). If too much pressure is applied, the artery can be occluded completely and no pulse felt. If you have difficulty finding these arteries, or feeling a pulse, ask your vet to demonstrate.

The digital artery is the other site at which you may feel for a pulse, particularly in lame horses. Two digital arteries supply each foot, and they can be felt just under the skin in the area directly above the bulb of each heel. If you run your fingers back along the side of the pastern (*see* Fig. 17), a tubular structure can be felt just as the fingers change direction to move round to the back of the pastern. In

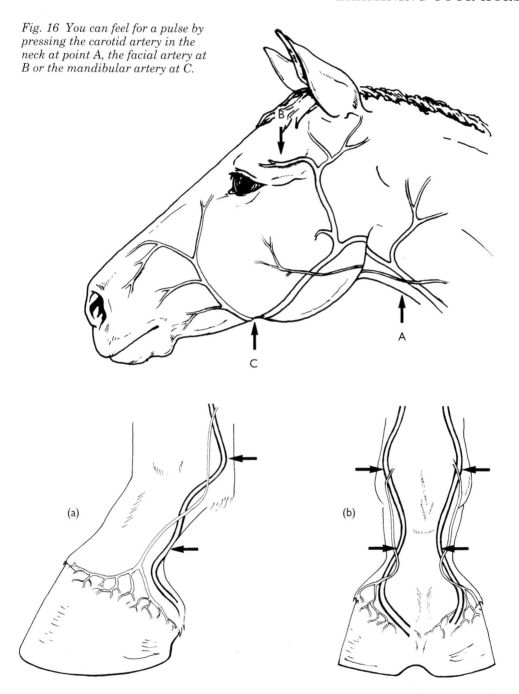

Fig. 16 You can feel for a pulse by pressing the carotid artery in the neck at point A, the facial artery at B or the mandibular artery at C.

Fig. 17 In the foot, you can locate the palmar digital arteries either at the fetlock (a) or on either side of the back of the pastern (b).

33

most horses a pulse cannot be felt here if there is no problem in the foot. The presence of inflammation, such as that caused by laminitis, by an infection such as a subsolar abscess, or by a fracture within the hoof, will give rise to an increased, and palpable, pulse to the foot.

Breathing Rate

In the normal horse, the respiratory rate at rest is 10 to 20 breaths per minute. This can be elevated after exercise, or as a result of pain or respiratory or heart disease. The respiratory rate can be counted by watching the movements of the chest wall. When horses are having difficulty breathing, or are tired after exercise, the walls of the abdomen as well as the chest will be seen moving with respiration.

Fear can also increase respiratory and heart rates, so abnormally high values may be obtained from frightened or nervous horses, even if they are otherwise healthy.

Normal vital signs

Temperature: 98.5–100.5°F (37.0–38.0°C).

Pulse: 25–40 beats per minute.

Respiration: 10–20 breaths per minute.

The Circulation

The mucous membranes (such as the gums) should be a pale pink colour. Dull brownish, or purplish mucous membranes can indicate septicaemia or toxaemia (overwhelming infection or toxin release by bacteria), as can 'injection' of the mucous membranes, when the blood vessels become congested and can be clearly seen as dark red lines against the paler gum colour. Abnormally pale mucous

membranes indicate that the circulation is poor, which can be caused by heart or lung problems, dehydration or blood loss.

The capillary refill time also gives an indication of the state of the circulation. This is tested by applying finger pressure to an area of gum. When the finger is removed, the gum will remain blanched for a few seconds before the blood returns to the area and it resumes its normal pink colour. The time taken for normal colour to return is measured, and should be in the region of two to three seconds in normal horses.

In addition, the hydration status can be measured by assessing the elasticity of the skin. This can be done by taking a pinch of skin on the neck, and then letting it go; the skin should spring back to normal within a few seconds. If it retains a pinched form, i.e. tented up in a ridge, the horse is likely to be somewhat dehydrated.

The Skin

If injury to the skin is suspected, you will of course assess any obvious wounds (see Chapter 8). However, more subtle injuries may have no other apparent symptom than inflammation, which is indicated by a change in the temperature of the skin surface. This can be felt by smoothing your hands over the horse. As you do this you may notice slight swellings, or small areas of scabbiness or coat thinning. Skin damage may be indicated if reddening or bruising of the area is present.

The Abdomen

Assessment of gut sounds can be made by placing an ear to the horse's side. In normal horses the guts gurgle almost constantly. In horses with colic the gut sounds may be reduced or increased, and some horses that are in pain also have reduced gut sounds.

The Eyes

If obvious damage to the eyes is present the vet should be called immediately (*see* Chapter 7). However, more subtle eye problems may be initially investigated at home.

If you suspect that your horse may not be able to see well, you can test his vision by feinting a finger at the eye (whilst being careful to avoid touching the lashes) and seeing whether or not he blinks. Shining a pen torch at the eye may allow you to recognize signs such as cloudiness, or abnormalities within the eye. Don't be concerned by the presence of small spherical objects that resemble peppercorns and lie just above the pupils; these are called the corpora nigra and are perfectly normal. To test the responsiveness of the pupils, place the horse in a dark stable, and shine a torch towards the eyes. The pupils should widen in the dark and become narrower when lit.

FEET AND LIMBS

Signs of Lameness

Lameness is one of the most common signs of injury in a horse. In some cases it is very easy to recognize, but in others the signs are much milder (*see* Chapter 11 for more details). A severe lameness affecting only one leg gives rise to an obvious limp; however, where pain affects more than one limb, or where the source of pain is quite high in the limb, the signs may be less easy to appreciate.

Pain in a limb usually results in the affected horse bearing less weight on that limb, and for less time, than he bears weight on the sound limb. (This is most easily assessed by listening to the sounds of footfalls on a hard surface.) In many cases signs such as a head nod, or the foot being raised to a lesser degree than the others, may also be seen. A lower than normal foot flight is most often seen in horses with joint problems, such as arthritis, that reduce their ability to lift the feet high off the ground.

When riding a lame horse, you may notice an obvious lurching movement. A less obviously lame horse may feel merely unlevel, or may be unable to lead on both diagonals, or (usually in the case of hind-limb lameness) to unite properly in canter.

The best way to assess whether or not a horse is lame is to watch him being led away from you, and then back towards you, over a distance of 20 yards (18m) or so. This should be done twice, on a firm, level surface, first at a walk and then at a trot. Watching a lame horse being lunged can also be helpful since moving in a circle forces the horse to bear weight asymmetrically, which can exacerbate the lameness. Most types of lameness show up most obviously when the affected leg is innermost on a circle and thus bearing proportionally more weight, while other types of lameness may show up most when the affected leg is on the outside. Lungeing a horse can be particularly helpful in the assessment of horses that are lame bilaterally, since lungeing may, for instance, make them appear first to be lamest on the left leg when working on a left-hand circle, but then lamest on the right leg when moving on a right-hand circle.

Forelimb lameness is usually indicated by head nodding: as weight is borne on the sore leg, the horse tenses to reduce the amount of weight passing through this limb, and this causes him to lift his head up; the head then nods down as the sound leg bears weight. Hind-limb lameness can be more difficult to assess as there is usually no head nod. Instead, the hindquarters tense and lift as the weight is borne on the painful leg, and drop as the sound leg bears weight.

Not all apparent lamenesses are caused by pain. Some conditions, or conformational abnormalities, can reduce the ability of the limb to move in a normal manner and so produce an abnormal gait that appears to be pain related. These so-called mechanical lamenesses should also be assessed.

Limb Examination

If you are not absolutely sure whether your horse is lame, start your investigations by examining his limbs carefully. Any mud should be brushed away, and the skin should be examined thoroughly for signs of wounds. At the same time, the joints should be felt, and any signs of swelling or heat noted. Running a hand over the tendon area, whilst feeling for swelling, heat and pain, is also advisable (see Chapter 11).

Inflammation results in the enlargement of the blood vessels in the immediate proximity of a wound or otherwise damaged tissue. This causes an increase in the blood supply to the affected area, resulting in swelling and an increase in heat. These signs can be difficult to recognize, especially if the swelling is not marked, and so they are best appreciated if the legs are compared; differences between the sound one and the lame one may then be more easily identified.

Having felt the limbs whilst the horse is standing on them, it can be helpful to lift the affected leg and feel the structures with the strain taken off it. Subtle swellings – in the tendon area, for instance – may thus become easy to recognize. In addition, the joints may be manipulated (bent and flexed), and any signs of pain this elicits may be used to assist you in making a diagnosis.

Back Examination

Most cases of lameness are related to the lower limbs; muscle spasm in the back, when present, is usually a secondary problem produced when the horse tenses his back in order to try to take his weight off the sore leg. Primary back pain does occur, though, and is often associated with poor saddle fit. Pain in the back (see Chapters 6 and 11) causes symptoms ranging from bilateral hind-limb lameness, poor hind-limb propulsion and decreased performance, to the development of a 'cold' back (when the horse tenses his back up, or dips it away, when saddled or mounted) or stiff back. Back pain can also cause discomfort during grooming and saddling up.

Assessment of back pain or tension can be made by running your hand down the horse's spine, and down the muscles on both sides of the spine. If the horse resents being touched in a particular area, or if asymmetry or warmth is found, a back problem may be suspected.

The flexibility of a horse's back can also be assessed (see Chapter 6) by running a sharpish object (such as the pointed lid of a pen) down both sides of the spine and checking that the horse bends away from the stimulus. In addition, pinching the horse's underside in the girth area should cause him to arch his back away from the stimulus. Horses with back pain generally guard against such movements.

Signs of disease

Signs of disease may be very obvious, such as when a horse collapses (see Chapter 5), has an open wound (see Chapter 8), has difficulty breathing, or can't walk. However, signs of more subtle disease can be difficult to recognize. When in doubt, call your vet.

---

3 First Aid: The Principles ──────

First and foremost, first aid means making a practical and sensible assessment of the situation.

The aims of any first-aid treatment are:

- To maintain life.
- To prevent worsening of a condition.
- To promote recovery.

It is important to have these principles in mind when approaching an injured horse. Bear in mind that in some situations the course of action that immediately suggests itself to you is not necessarily the best one, so it is important to take a mental step back from an emergency, and to remain calm and think clearly about the implications of the possible options.

A situation that requires urgent veterinary attention should be identified as such immediately and the vet contacted. Whilst awaiting the vet, further assessment may be carried out, and, where it is safe to do so, appropriate first-aid treatment applied. If a situation does not demand urgent veterinary attention, it is useful to be able to differentiate between a problem that requires same-day or next-day veterinary treatment, and one that you, the owner, can deal with. There is nothing more frustrating for a vet than having to treat an injury that, had it been seen a few days earlier, would have saved the horse unnecessary pain and distress, and would have been easier and cheaper to treat.

In many cases a horse will have more than one type of injury present, or potentially present, and one of the most important things to decide is which injury is the one that needs to be prioritized. In addition, it is necessary to remember that however distressing a situation is, the first priority is to deal with any injured people, and the second is to prevent the injury of any first-aiders or helpers.

INITIAL ASSESSMENT

Some emergency situations are instantly recognizable as such. These include those in which a horse is trapped or cannot rise, or is unable to bear weight on a limb, or is in severe pain or distress. Other situations can ultimately be just as life-threatening, such as wounds in the vicinity of joints or tendon sheaths, and severe bleeding.

Where possible the entire horse should be examined, and all injuries noted. However, if this is likely to cause further distress to the horse, or if any obviously severe injuries are present, examination of the horse may be postponed until the vet is present. Few injuries necessitate immediate attention in the meantime, and attempts to intervene inappropriately in emergency situations can cause the horse unnecessary distress and exacerbate the problem. The exception to this is wounds that are bleeding copiously, which should have pressure dressings applied (*see* Chapter 4).

Priorities

1. Assess the situation. Can the horse be safely approached; and, if so, how?

2. Assess the injuries that are present. Control any bleeding.

3. Decide whether immediate veterinary attention is necessary – i.e., is the horse unable to rise, unable to bear weight on a limb, in severe pain or distress, or bleeding severely?

4. Initiate emergency treatment where appropriate and safe to do so. Ensure any bleeding is under control. Prevent further injury. Clean wounds where appropriate.

5. Decide if/when less urgent veterinary attention is needed. Assess for signs of shock. Assess position of any wounds to rule out the possibility of involvement of a joint or tendon sheath.

It is helpful to be able to distinguish between arterial and venous bleeding. The arteries are the blood vessels that carry blood from the heart to the body, and they pump blood out in time with each heart beat. This means that where major arteries are involved in wounds, spurts of blood may be seen, and large amounts of blood can be lost quickly. Severe blood loss can be fatal. Venous bleeding, however, is usually less serious. Blood in the veins is at low pressure as it returns from the organs of the body to the heart. Because the pressure in the veins is lower than that in the arteries, and they are not directly connected to the heart, blood from damaged veins tends to seep or ooze, rather than gush or spurt, and the blood may well clot on its own. A horse is unlikely to bleed to death from a damaged vein, but can do so from an arterial wound.

If a horse that has been injured does not initially appear to be badly or seriously hurt, a full examination of the sites of any wounds can allow assessment of the likelihood of any of these wounds involving a joint or tendon sheath. This is important because if infection of joints or tendon-sheaths develops following contamination of a wound in the area, it can be unresponsive to treatment, and so prove fatal. A good working knowledge of your horse's basic anatomy is therefore of paramount importance (*see* Figs 2–3 and 46–47). As a rule of thumb, any wounds that overlie joints, or are anywhere on the hind surface of the lower limbs (thus potentially involving the main tendons), necessitate urgent veterinary attention however innocuous they appear. This includes solar wounds, particularly those involving nail penetrations through the sole, since these may involve the coffin joint, the navicular bone, and the distal end of the deep digital-flexor tendon. If veterinary attention in any of these cases is postponed beyond four or six hours of the injury, irreversible infection may already be present when the vet arrives.

CALLING THE VET

It is extremely important not only to be able to assess a situation calmly and sensibly, but also to be able to communicate the nature of it – and the degree of urgency it constitutes – to your vet or the surgery's reception staff. If the vet knows what to expect, he will be better equipped to deal with the situation on arrival. Even if you are not sure how much of an emergency a given situation constitutes, a clear description of a horse's condition is still very important in order to enable the vet to assess its seriousness and respond accordingly.

Before you call the veterinary practice, make sure you are able to describe precisely where you are and, where possible, provide a contact telephone number. If you have a mobile phone, give that number (even if your vet usually has it on record); if not, try to give the number of a nearby telephone and, where possible, leave someone by the phone in case the vet needs to call you back. On calling the surgery, give the person who answers the telephone your name, and the full address of the premises; even if you are at the horse's usual premises, and the vet you usually see knows exactly where this is, give concise directions. If you have it, a six-figure Ordnance Survey map reference can also be helpful.

Whilst awaiting the vet, your priorities are to prevent the situation worsening and to avoid human injury. Keep these in mind at all times. If there is time, it is worth contacting your insurance company at this stage to notify them that an injury has occurred, and that veterinary attention is necessary, as prompt notification can facilitate your claim.

Defining an emergency

Is your horse:

- Unable to rise?

- Unable to balance?

- Unable to bear any weight on a leg?

- In severe pain or distress?

- Wounded, with pumping blood or possible damage to joints or tendon sheaths?

- Attempting without success to give birth?

If the answer to any of these questions is yes, emergency veterinary attention should be sought.

FURTHER ASSESSMENT AND TREATMENT

Even if a horse is badly injured, a basic examination can usually be carried out, and the results of this may be helpful to the vet when he arrives. However, it is worth repeating that if examining the horse would cause him further pain or distress, or would put human helpers at risk, it is better not to examine the horse. If, on the other hand, your initial assessment has led you to believe that veterinary attention is not necessary, or is not urgent, a prompt detailed examination is particularly important. If this uncovers signs that the injuries are more severe than was initially thought, the vet can then be contacted.

On arrival at an emergency situation, your vet will first need to assess the severity of the horse's condition. If necessary, the vet will sedate or anaesthetize the horse so that further assessment or treatment can be carried out, and painkillers and other appropriate treatment such as antibiotics can be administered. Dressings and bandages may need to be removed and reapplied; and, where fractures are diagnosed or suspected, support bandages or a splint may need to be applied. The vet can then decide whether further treatment should be carried out, or whether referral is necessary, or whether, in the case of non-treatable injuries, euthanasia is necessary.

Restraint

As discussed above, it may be necessary to restrain a horse in order to examine him, or to make an assessment of a situation, or to permit you to apply first aid. This in itself may require the attention of a veterinary surgeon, and where it is dangerous for helpers to approach the horse, a vet should be awaited; handling of the horse should be avoided until appropriate medication such as sedatives or tranquillizers can be given. In the case of the trapped or down horse, struggling and attempts to rise should be prevented if possible and safe to do so. Most horses can be kept lying on their sides by one or two people applying their weight to the upper neck, and in some cases this may be appropriate. Hobbles and ropes can be used to aid control or movement of a horse (*see* Chapter 5), but the application of these in the conscious and unsedated horse is not to be recommended as they

may cause further struggling. Where the level of pain or distress is not too great, temporary restraint may be achieved by applying a twitch to the upper lip (*see* Fig. 18), wrapping the lead rope around the nose, or by gripping a fold of skin on the neck.

Transporting an Injured Horse

In the UK, the regulations governing the transport of an injured horse (to a referral centre, for example) are laid down in leg-

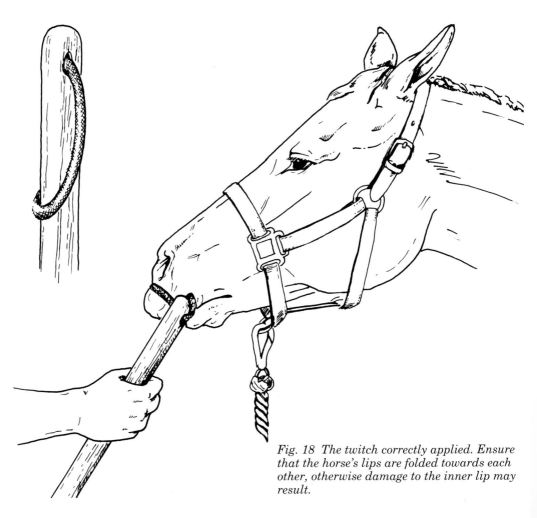

Fig. 18 The twitch correctly applied. Ensure that the horse's lips are folded towards each other, otherwise damage to the inner lip may result.

islation. This proscribes the transport of an animal that is unfit for travel owing to disease, infirmity, illness, injury, fatigue, or any other reason. A vet is the only person qualified to decide if an animal injured at home or at an event is fit to travel, and the only one who has the right to enforce his opinion on the matter.

Injured horses may be transported to the nearest place that is able to offer appropriate treatment, but where the dragging or lifting of such horses is necessary to effect this, transport must take place under veterinary supervision. Depending on such criteria as the distance to be travelled, it may be necessary for the vet to issue a certificate that allows for such transport.

Preparation for transport includes the application of appropriate dressings and protective boots, and suitable bedding of the lorry or trailer. Where necessary, a horse may be sedated for such a journey. In transporting an injured horse, it is important for the driver of the box or trailer to be skilled, and to avoid unnecessary stress of the horse during transport. The vet should ensure that the driver also has full directions to the destination.

EUTHANASIA

Although it is not a pleasant subject to consider, it is a fact that some equine injuries are not treatable, and for such injuries euthanasia may be the only option.

Horses that are not going to recover from their injuries, and should therefore be euthanased, include horses with untreatable fractures, neurological (nervous) disease, and joint or synovial sheath (e.g. tendon) injuries.

If a horse is insured, the insurance company should be contacted for authorization before euthanasia is carried out; otherwise, subsequent claims may not be met.

The exception to this is cases where horses are in severe and unremitting pain, and immediate euthanasia on humane grounds is necessary. (In such cases, it is important to have written confirmation of this from your vet.)

Untreatable fractures (*see* Chapter 11), for the most part, include those involving the femur (the thigh bone), the tibia (the main bone between the stifle and the hock), and the humerus of adult horses (between the shoulder and the elbow). Any fractures in which there are many fragments with accompanying severe tissue damage may also necessitate euthanasia.

Horses with neurological disease that cannot be treated include most of those that are conscious but recumbent (unable to rise) and make no attempt to rise after one hour, those that are paralysed for two to four hours or more with no signs of improvement, those in a coma for more than 24 to 48 hours, and those in uncontrollable pain.

A horse that is suffering from severe and unremitting pain for other reasons, such as uncontrollable infection of joints, tendon sheaths, or other synovial structures, may also need to be euthanased. Those horses whose owners cannot afford appropriate treatment are better euthanased early in the course of a disease, before they have suffered too much, than subjected to treatment that holds no chance of recovery.

Methods of Euthanasia, and Disposal

Where horses are suffering unremitting pain, the only consideration should be the speed with which that pain can be alleviated. However, there are inherent problems with the disposal of horses' bodies after death; and these considerations may determine the method of euthanasia. In addition, the injury from which the horse is suffering may preclude the use of certain methods of euthanasia.

Collection and disposal of a horse's body can be carried out by a huntsman or horse slaughterer (in which case the body is usually used to feed dogs), or by pet crematoria that are licensed for this purpose. Cremation, which is expensive but nevertheless favoured by many owners, can be organized privately by the owner of the horse, or through the veterinary surgeon. The third option is burial, which can be carried out on the owner's premises, with permission from the relevant authority (in the UK the Environment Agency), and merely requires access to a digger to dig the grave. If there are any queries about the siting of the grave, seek advice from the relevant authority.

Euthanasia is usually carried out either by lethal injection or with a gun of the type used for humane slaughter. For many owners, the use of a gun is extremely upsetting, and lethal injection is preferred. Certainly the death of a horse by shooting seems somehow more brutal, as horses tend to fall to the ground very hard, and afterwards there may be some twitching owing to muscle reflexes. In addition, some bleeding may be seen. However, from the horse's point of view, the gun may well be preferable since

death from shooting is instantaneous, and the horse is unaware of any reflex behaviour that he may show after death. Euthanasia by humane injection often involves the placement of an intravenous catheter, through which the lethal substance is given. After its injection there is often a period of a few seconds during which the horse appears sleepy, and then there may be a brief excitation phase during which the horse will sometimes lift his head slightly, and even whinny, just before he dies. Again some reflex movements may be seen after death, and it may take a few minutes for the heart to stop.

Euthanasia by lethal injection should not be carried out in horses with any history of epilepsy, as fitting can occur during the excitation phase in these horses. Whether using a gun, or a lethal injection, horses that are excitable, difficult to handle, or in extreme pain should first be sedated to avoid difficulties.

Horses that have been euthanased by lethal injection must be buried or cremated; horse slaughterers and huntsmen can only take bodies of horses that have been euthanased by shooting. In rare cases where horses are lethally wounded but cannot be caught, they may first need to be sedated by dart-gun. In the UK, only vets licensed by the Home Office may use a dart-gun.

4 First Aid: The Practice ——————

THE FIRST-AID EXAMINATION

The basic first-aid examination is covered in more detail in Chapter 2 but it is worth reiterating the five main points:

1. Check the gum colour. The pink colour should return within five seconds of blanching the gum with finger pressure.
2. Check the heart rate by placing a hand directly over the heart or onto the pulse in the maxillary artery as it crosses the jaw bone. A normal resting heart rate is 25 to 40 beats per minute.
3. Check respiration by counting the horse's breaths, which should be 10 to 20 per minute at rest.
4. Listen for gut noise on both sides of the abdomen.
5. Take the temperature using a rectal thermometer. The horse's temperature should be 99.8–100.5°F (37.6–38°C).

The results of such an examination should, if possible, be recorded on paper, as should the time at which this and subsequent examinations are carried out. When any horse has been injured, however mildly, the recording of temperature, pulse and respiration at least twice daily can aid recognition of early signs of secondary problems such as infections.

When carrying out an examination, look out for signs of shock. Shock is a clinical condition that occurs when the body reacts to trauma; it is not necessarily precipitated by 'fright'. Symptoms of shock include low temperature (hypothermia), a fast, weak pulse and an increased breathing rate, and may also include wobbliness or collapse, and trembling. A horse suffering from shock should be wrapped in warm rugs and blankets) should be kept as quiet as possible, and should be seen by a vet promptly. Intravenous fluid therapy may prove necessary in some cases.

Increased pulse and breathing rates, can be a sign of shock, or blood loss, but can also simply be a sign that the affected horse is in some pain or distress. Decreased pulse and breathing rates can indicate that the horse's level of consciousness is deteriorating.

Elevated core temperatures (hyperthermia) can occur as a result of infection or inflammation, or indeed through pain or exhaustion (after endurance work, for example). In such cases the most appropriate treatment is the application of large amounts of cold water to the horse's body to encourage cooling.

Urgent Cases

A number of conditions demand prompt examination by a vet. These include eye injuries, nervous diseases, difficulty in breathing, nasal discharge containing blood or pus, high temperature, and ingestion of poisonous plants. Insect stings and

---

The first-aid kit

A basic first-aid kit should include:

- Paper and a pen or pencil.
- A thermometer.
- A clean bowl.
- Wire cutters.
- Scissors.
- Tweezers.
- Selection of clean syringes.
- Sterile water/saline.
- Antiseptic solution: povidone iodine or chlorhexidine.
- Anti-bacterial dusting powder for skin wounds (obtained from your vet).
- Antiseptic spray (obtained from your vet).
- Intrasite, or similar gel, with which to pack a cleaned open wound to avoid bacterial proliferation.
- Sticky tape for anchoring dressings or bandages.
- Cotton wool, gamgee.

- Animalintex for poulticing.
- Sterile non-adherent dressings (e.g. Melolin).
- Different types of medical bandage:

  Soft padding bandages (e.g. Softban), or a roll of gamgee or cotton wool.

  Net/gauze bandages (e.g. K-Ban), which can be used to anchor a dressing, or apply some pressure over a thick padding layer.

  Self-adherent, stretchy bandages (e.g. Vetrap and Elastoplast), which can be used to anchor and protect lower layers of bandages.

- Stable bandages (tail bandages are particularly useful) for applying support when used over a thick padding layer or for anchoring temporary dressings.
- Petroleum jelly.
- Fly repellent.
- Basic medication appropriate for your horse as discussed with your vet.

---

snake bites may also require prompt treatment. In addition, there are the emergency situations listed in Chapter 3, which are considered in more detail here.

EMERGENCIES

Collapse or Inability to Rise

Horses rarely suffer sudden collapse (*see* Chapter 5), but when they do – whether through heart problems, breathing difficulties, epilepsy, or injury – they require rapid attention. If the horse is still down, try to keep him still and calm if it is safe for you to do so. If the horse has risen, it is probably better to await the vet than to try to move the animal. If he is unconscious or partly conscious, or has other signs of nervous-system injuries, it is important to check that he is able to breathe in the position he's in, and that the airway is clear and not blocked with blood or mucus. While waiting for the vet to arrive, you can conduct a variety of tests to assess the status of the horse (*see* Chapter 5).

Non-weight-bearing Lameness

If a horse cannot bear weight on a limb, or has extreme difficulty doing so (*see*

Chapter 11), then it is best not to move the animal while waiting for the vet in case a fracture is present. First aid is best avoided unless there are wounds that require attention.

Severe Pain or Distress

Any situation that is causing a horse distress should be investigated promptly. Although reproductive problems will not be discussed in detail here, any difficulties in foaling constitute an emergency (*see* Chapter 10), as does priapism (sustained erection) in the male. If the penis is left unretracted it can easily become damaged, and if not treated promptly this can mean that the stallion is unable to serve mares in the future.

Even mild abdominal pain/colic (*see* Chapter 10) should be investigated by a vet, as progression of the underlying cause can easily give rise to a more severe problem that is more difficult to treat. Whilst awaiting the vet, encouraging the animal to walk around may help to ease the pain. It is unlikely that allowing a horse to roll will cause twists in the gut, but rolling should be avoided, particularly in an area where the horse could become cast.

In most cases of choke (blockage of the oesophagus), the blockage clears by the time the vet arrives. However, choke must still be considered an emergency because it is potentially fatal (*see* Chapter 9). Horses with choke are found in extreme distress with food material and saliva discharging from the nostrils, and difficulty in breathing. The horse may also stand with the neck stretched forward. Reassurance (and withdrawal of further food – some horses will continue to attempt to eat!) is all that can be done until the vet arrives, when sedation and the insertion of a stomach tube into the oesophagus is usually successful in clearing the blockage.

Wounds

Not all wounds will need immediate veterinary attention, but wounds that have any of the following characteristics constitute an emergency and should be treated by a vet without delay:

- Pouring or pumping blood.
- Leaking joint fluid (straw-coloured and viscous liquid).
- Situated in the vicinity of the joints or tendon sheaths.
- A foreign body (for example, a stake) is known or suspected to be involved.

Where it is safe to do so, a sterile dressing and a clean bandage (*see* bandaging, page 46) should be applied to stop bleeding. If blood continues to seep through, further layers of bandage can be applied; do not disturb the first layers. Firm bandaging will stop or ease bleeding until the vet arrives.

If a foreign body is involved, be careful not to push it further into the wound when bandaging (*see* Fig. 27). If the horse is still attached to a foreign body, it may be possible to cut it as close to the horse as possible. Do not attempt to remove the article until the vet arrives, and try not to move the horse.

Any wound (*see* Chapter 8) can become infected, and those on the limbs usually do. Whenever the skin is broken, infection can result and tetanus antitoxin treatment may be necessary. Veterinary attention within four to six hours is optimal, particularly if it is likely that the wound will require suturing, or if there is any likelihood that deep structures such as joints and tendons are involved. Further delay increases the chance that a wound that was initially merely contaminated will become infected as bacteria reproduce. This will then necessitate more treatment, can increase the chance of wound breakdown after stitching, and can

45

be catastrophic where joints or tendon sheaths are involved.

Dirty wounds may be cleaned with a 0.1 per cent povidone iodine (1 measure of Pevidine scrub in 7.5 measures water) or 0.05 per cent chlorhexidine (1 measure of Hibiscrub in 40 measures of water) solution (*see* pages 88 and 89) and poulticed with Animalintex soaked in warm water. They should not be hosed as this can force bacteria deeper. Any horse with a wound should be brought in and box-rested until examined by a vet.

Solar punctures also require prompt veterinary attention as they generally do become infected. If a shoe has come loose, rotated and been trodden on, it should be removed, if possible, to prevent further damage. If a nail is found stuck into the foot, the vet should be called urgently, and the nail should be left alone until he arrives (unless to do so would cause the horse further pain or distress, or would cause the nail to become more deeply embedded). If the nail is left in situ, the vet can better assess the position and extent of the puncture wounds and thus what deeper structures may be involved. The foot should be tubbed in salt water (1 teaspoon salt to 1 pint water), covered to prevent further contamination, and poulticed with Animalintex.

Swellings

When swellings on the limbs occur, particularly if with concurrent lameness, cold hosing/cold packing and bandaging of the area is indicated (ice-packs are not a good idea as they can cause freeze burns to the skin). Box-rest on soft bedding is advisable, particularly if tendon damage (*see* Chapter 11) is suspected, and it is important to apply a support bandage (*see* bandaging below) to the unaffected limb to prevent damage that may result from the increased strain that it is bearing.

Lameness

One of the other causes of lameness that necessitates a veterinary visit is laminitis (*see* Chapter 11). Where bilateral forelimb lameness is seen with heat in the feet and increased pulse in the digital arteries (*see* Fig. 17), box-rest on soft bedding and reduction of food intake should be instituted. Exercise is not a good idea, neither is cold hosing nor hot tubbing of the feet. Any other lameness problem of acute onset is best seen by a vet sooner rather than later, and box-rest in the meantime is always a good idea.

BANDAGING TECHNIQUES

On the whole, bandages are applied for one, or several, of four reasons. These comprise:

1. To staunch or reduce bleeding.
2. To keep a wound clean, covered and protected from infection.
3. To prevent or control swelling.
4. To provide support to an area.

Before applying a bandage, it is important to decide which of these reasons apply, and to select the bandage that is properly fit for the purpose. In addition, it is essential to ensure the following: that bandages are not applied so tightly that they cause damage to underlying tissues; that they are applied with even pressure throughout; and that they are changed frequently. To maintain even pressure while bandaging, check that the bandage overlaps half of the previous layer. If bandages are too tight, the skin underneath can become sore, and may ulcerate. If this happens the area will become painful, and the horse may try to remove his dressings. In addition, swelling above the bandage may be seen.

The Pressure Bandage

This is used to staunch or reduce bleeding (*see* Fig. 19).

If a wound is bleeding copiously, it may be necessary to apply a pressure bandage in order to control the bleeding whilst awaiting the vet. Examples of wounds requiring a pressure bandage would include lower limb wounds involving arteries.

In such cases, a non-adherent sterile dressing should be applied directly over the wound, and anchored in place with a crepe or gauze bandage. Over this, a soft conforming layer such as cotton wool, Softban or gamgee is needed to allow pressure to be applied without causing damage to the surrounding skin. A gauze or crepe bandage can be applied over this to exert pressure, and further layers of cotton wool and gauze can be applied to increase the pressure and support exerted. This means that direct pressure to the skin is not applied, which helps avoid the development of pressure sores.

If bleeding continues, further layers of soft conforming cotton wool-type dressings covered with tight pressure wraps should be applied over the top until the bleeding ceases. If bleeding ceases, or the bandage has been *in situ* for more than an hour, it is a good idea to loosen it slightly in order to allow some blood flow to the area to return. Vetrap or Elastoplast can be applied on the outside of these layers, if necessary, to keep them clean and dry.

If a wound is bleeding copiously, but is in such a position that a bandage cannot be applied, the blood flow should be stemmed by exerting pressure by hand. To do this, a clean, absorbent pad, such as a clean towel, should be pressed into or against the wound and held there until the vet arrives.

Where a pressure bandage is used, it really needs to be applied to the whole of the limb below the wound, as well as to the area of the wound itself. Pressure bandages that are localized to an area in the middle of a limb can cause swelling of the limb below the dressing as the pressure of the bandage prevents the blood in the area returning to the body. This can cause discomfort and, ultimately, swelling of the area of the injury, which may slow its healing. It is also important not to have the edge of a pressure bandage overlying the tendon area, as this can cause pressure-related damage to the underlying tendons. Instead, it is far preferable to extend the bandage to the joint above, to allow equal pressure to be exerted over the whole tendon area.

Pressure bandages always run the risk of causing damage to the underlying skin, by reducing the blood supply to this area. They should never be applied for more than two to four hours unless prescribed by your vet, and, in the minority of cases where they do need to be used for two to three days, they must be changed on a daily basis by the vet to avoid causing skin excoriation.

The Support Bandage

This is used to protect or support the limb, to prevent excess movement of an injured joint, and to dissipate lower limb swelling (*see* Fig. 20).

The application of support bandages is similar to that of pressure bandages. When long-term severe injuries are present, they result in the horse resting the injured limb for some of the time so that it thus bears comparatively less weight. The contralateral (opposite) limb, which is therefore bearing comparatively more weight, should have a support bandage applied to prevent it developing a tendon

47

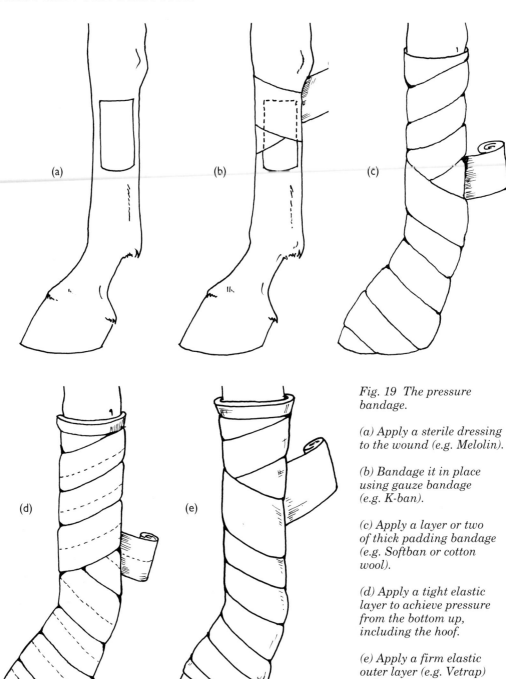

(a)

(b)

(c)

(d)

(e)

Fig. 19 The pressure bandage.

(a) Apply a sterile dressing to the wound (e.g. Melolin).

(b) Bandage it in place using gauze bandage (e.g. K-ban).

(c) Apply a layer or two of thick padding bandage (e.g. Softban or cotton wool).

(d) Apply a tight elastic layer to achieve pressure from the bottom up, including the hoof.

(e) Apply a firm elastic outer layer (e.g. Vetrap) to keep dressings clean and dry.

Fig. 20 The support bandage.

(a) Apply a gamgee or foam pad.

(b) Bandage it in place with firm elastic bandage, such as exercise or tail bandage.

(a)

(b)

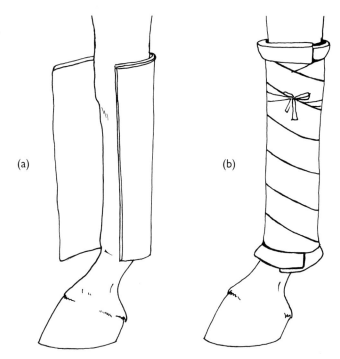

injury. In some cases frog supports are also applied to prevent the development of laminitis (*see* Chapter 11). Support bandages are also needed when tendon damage has occurred, or is suspected, and the same kind of bandaging techniques can be used to apply temporary bandages to reduce swellings (filling) of the lower limbs, and to prevent excess movements of the limbs that can delay healing of a wound in the vicinity of a joint.

The easiest way to apply a support dressing is to use a large pad of gamgee and wrap it round the lower limb from above the knee to below the fetlock. A firm layer of elastic bandage is then applied, again from the knee or above, to below the fetlock. These bandages should be changed at least twice daily to prevent the development of skin excoriation.

Where bandages are needed over joints or bony prominences, methods must be employed to avoid pressure sores. These include cutting through the bandage where it overlies specific pressure points, such as the point of the elbow or hock, or the accessory carpal bone (Fig. 21) on the back of the knee. It is also important never to have the edge of a pressure or support bandage overlying the tendon area, as this can cause pressure-related damage to the underlying tendons. Instead, it is preferable to continue the bandage to incorporate the whole of the tendon area so that the same pressure is applied throughout, and to ensure that these bandages are well padded to avoid direct pressure.

Firm support dressings can also be used to protect the fractured or badly injured limb from further damage, and to

49

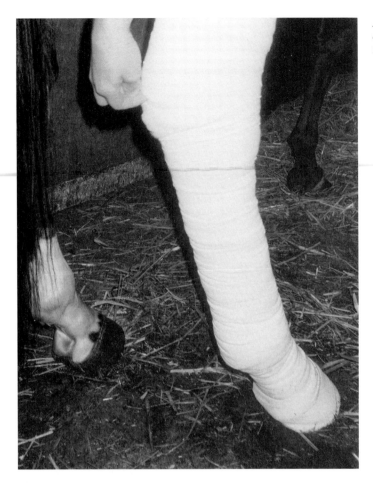

Fig. 21 Cutting the bandage over the point of the hock to relieve pressure.

reduce pain. This can be especially useful if a horse with a fractured (or possibly fractured) limb needs to be transported to an equine hospital for further treatment. In such cases, it is important to prevent excessive movement in the limb during transit, and so the vet will apply a very firm, multi-layered support bandage to the affected limb in order to keep it in a secure position. Such a bandage is commonly known as a Robert Jones bandage (*see* Chapter 11). If applied properly it can provide the same support as would a cast. In some cases a splint is also incorporated.

The Basic Bandage

This is used to keep a wound protected (*see* Fig. 22).

Bandaging of wounds, rather than leaving them open, is to be recommended. Not only does it help to keep the wound clean and to protect it from contamination and further injury, but it prevents the wound from drying out too much, which can slow healing.

Wounds on the body are usually difficult to dress, but wounds on the limbs (which is where wounds most commonly

Fig. 22 Bandaging a dressing in place in the vicinity of a joint – the figure-of-eight bandage.

(a) Apply a sterile dressing, and secure it with gauze bandage.

(b) Bandage in a figure of eight around the joint to anchor the dressing. Use further layers of padding material and gauze as necessary.

(c) Apply a firm elastic layer to keep the dressings clean and dry.

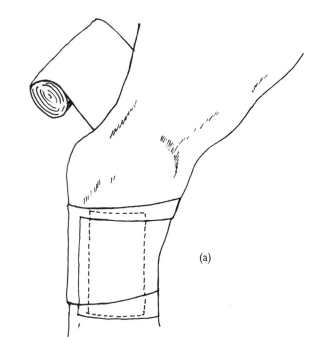

(a)

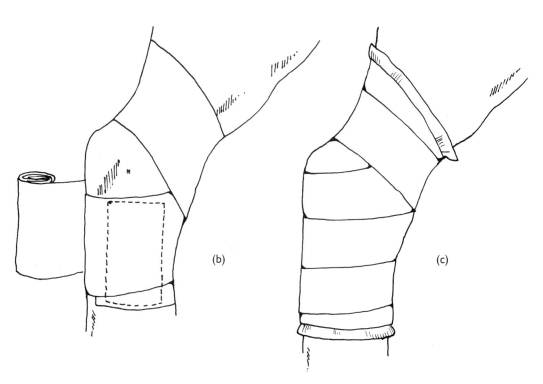

(b)

(c)

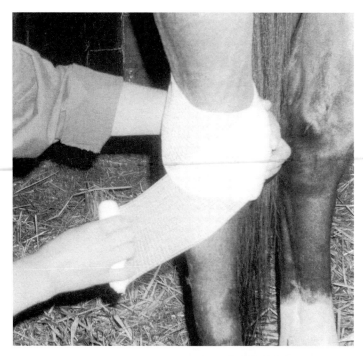

Fig. 23 Bandaging the hock.

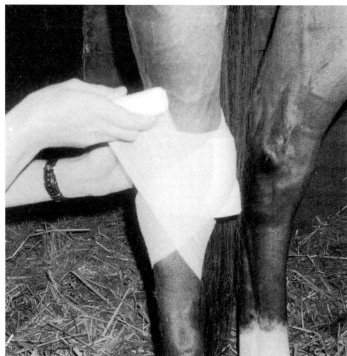

Fig. 24 Creating the figure-of-eight formation.

Fig. 25 To prevent swelling, the bandage is being extended to include the lower part of the limb.

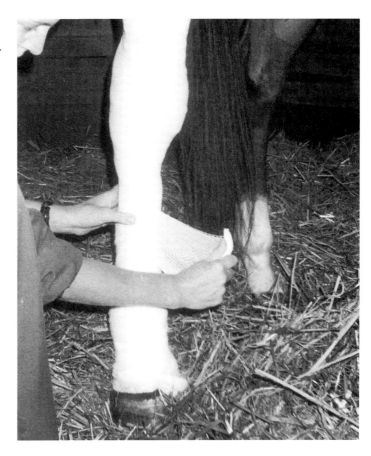

occur) can usually be bandaged relatively easily. The most difficult consideration is usually how to prevent such dressings from slipping.

In most cases, the wound should first be cleaned with a dilute antiseptic solution (*see* pages 88 and 89) before applying a sterile dressing. The dressing is usually bandaged in place with a non-adherent, stretch-bandage material, such as crepe or gauze, which is then held in place by a stronger, self-adhesive bandage such as 'Vetrap', or a washable elastic bandage. To avoid slipping, the bandage is usually applied in a figure-of-eight manner (*see* Figs 22–24) to anchor it to the nearest joint, and a layer of Elastoplast may then

be used to anchor it to the skin and hair. This method is ideal for covering a wound whilst the horse is awaiting veterinary attention. Such bandages are best applied firmly but not tightly. and should be changed at least once daily.

If a dressing of this type needs to be left on longer than a single day, padding material must be incorporated to avoid pressure sores developing. The sterile dressing is still anchored in place with a crepe or gauze bandage, but then a layer of Softban, cotton wool or gamgee should be applied, and secured with a further layer of gauze or crepe. Vetrap or an elastic bandage may then be applied to protect the dressing, and self-adhesive bandage may

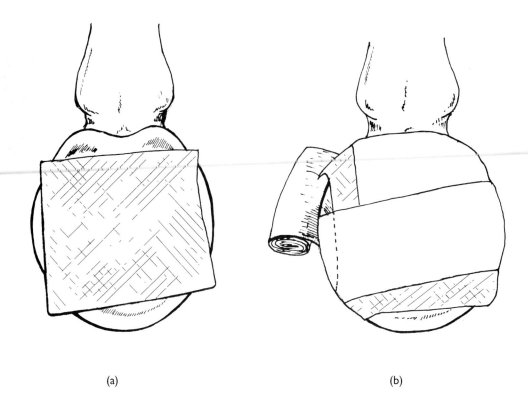

(a)   (b)

Fig. 26 Poulticing the foot. (a) Apply poulticing material (such as Animalintex soaked in warm water) to the affected area (i.e. the sole of the foot). (b) Bandage it in place with gauze dressing or elastic bandage. (c) If you have one, an Equiboot can be placed over the dressed foot to keep it clean and moist. (d) If you do not have an Equiboot, you can place the dressed foot into a thick plastic bag secured with more bandage.

be used to anchor it. To avoid swelling below the bandage, the padding may be extended to incorporate the lower part of the limb (Fig. 25). This type of dressing can be safely left in place for two to three days, and is ideal for longer-term management of a wound. It is important to apply sufficient padding, and to be careful not to bandage over the edges of this with the gauze or crepe, to ensure that the latter cannot cut into the skin. Zip-fastening knee and hock bandages are available and

can be used for anchoring dressings in these areas.

The Poultice

This is used for special cases, such as foot wounds, in which infection is present (*see* Fig. 26).

Poultices are used to help draw out infection from deep or puncture wounds. In

54

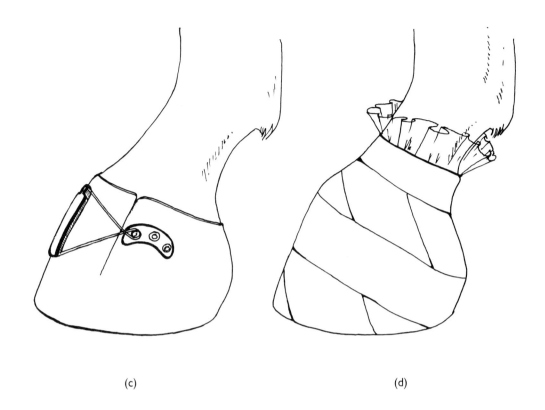

(c)   (d)

most situations, Animalintex soaked in hot – but not scalding – water, is appropriate. It should be applied twice daily to the wound (shiny plastic side away from the wound) and bandaged securely in place.

When bandaging on a poultice, the bandage needs to be firm enough to keep the poultice in place. Where wounds involve the foot, Animalintex can be secured with a strong, self-adhesive bandage, and a plastic cover can be taped in place to keep the dressing clean and moist. A rubbish bag folded into several layers and then taped around the fetlock can be used (*see* Fig. 26d), but a Reboboot or an Equiboot (*see* Fig. 26c) is better still.

If a foreign body such as a stake is present in a wound, it is important not to remove or disturb it until the vet arrives.

If the horse is still attached to the foreign body, try to cut the object off as close to the horse as can be achieved. If possible, such wounds are best left open and undisturbed until the vet arrives, but if such a wound is bleeding copiously, it can be bandaged in a figure of eight around the object (Fig. 27). It is important not to push the object further into the wound. If such a wound cannot be bandaged, pressure can be applied by hand using an absorbent pad such as a clean towel. Again, it is important not to disturb the foreign body in the process.

Horses that try to remove bandages that are correctly applied and not too tight can be prevented from doing so by using a cradle, a bib, or a muzzle, so that they cannot reach the area, or by painting the outer surface of the bandage with an unpleasant-tasting compound.

55

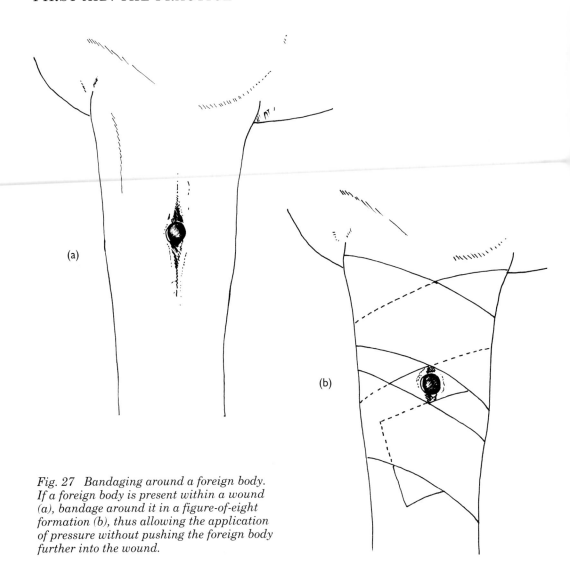

(a)

(b)

Fig. 27 Bandaging around a foreign body.
If a foreign body is present within a wound
(a), bandage around it in a figure-of-eight
formation (b), thus allowing the application
of pressure without pushing the foreign body
further into the wound.

Once the initial phase of healing has taken place, and the wounds are stable and granulating healthily rather than oozing fluid, it may be best to leave them open to the air. This allows them to dry out, and to scab over. Bandages may need to be used for a longer period on wounds in high-motion areas to prevent the development of proud flesh which can, if not treated appropriately, delay healing.

5 Collapse

There are a number of reasons why horses may collapse and have difficulty rising. Some of these may be immediately obvious, and others more difficult to determine. In some cases collapse follows an injury, or excessive exercise. If a horse has a history of collapsing, knowledge of it aids assessment of the horse, and diagnosis of the cause of his recumbency. In other cases horses are found in a state of collapse with no known cause; determination of the reason for this can be very much more difficult.

Some causes of collapse can be avoided by regular health checks, which allow recognition of any signs of heart or respiratory disease, or other conditions. Such problems may then be taken into account when planning the horse's management and workload. At the time of a horse's yearly vaccination you can ask your vet to examine him and to make an assessment of his general state of health and wellbeing. In addition, any signs of illness or loss of performance that crop up at other times should be promptly investigated by your vet before more serious symptoms develop. At many forms of advanced work (such as endurance work, and three-day events) veterinary checks allow monitoring of the horse's state of health and fitness. Ensuring your horse is fit enough for the type of work you are asking of him helps to avoid exhaustion and injury.

Horses that collapse after exercise or exertion (and this can include horses loose at pasture if they are stimulated to exert themselves), may simply be suffering from a form of exhaustion or, on hot days, from heatstroke. Alternatively, exertion may have caused sudden worsening of an underlying problem such as heart disease, or may have predisposed the horse to injury. Horses that are tired are more likely to stumble or fall than those that are still fresh, and thus are more likely to injure themselves in this manner.

EXAMINATION OF A RECUMBENT HORSE

In trying to discover the cause of recumbency, the vet will search for any signs of trauma, such as head or back injuries, or damage to the limbs. A basic clinical examination (see Chapter 2) aids assessment. If the heart and breathing rates are elevated, pain or exhaustion may be suspected. If the pulse is weak and thready, and the mucous membranes (gums) are pale, a heart problem, or internal bleeding, may be present. An increased rectal temperature may indicate heatstroke.

In all cases, urgent veterinary attention should be sought. In the meantime first-aid should be carried out where possible. This can be based on the human **ABC** (Airway, Breathing, Circulation) criteria.

1. The **airway** should first be assessed. This may involve straightening the neck, or stretching out the head; where necessary, the nostrils and mouth should be cleared of any matter.
2. The **breathing** should then be assessed and monitored.

57

3. The **circulation** should then be checked. This involves checking the heart rate and rhythm, as well as feeling the pulse to check that the heart is pumping normally (*see* Chapter 2). Looking at the colour of the mucous membranes (e.g. the gums) to check that they are nice and pink also aids assessment of the circulation (*see* Chapter 2).

After this, any further first-aid, such as applying pressure to bleeding wounds, can be carried out.

CAUSES OF COLLAPSE

Injury

This usually occurs as the result of an accident, such as falling or running into a jump or a fence. However, bony injuries such as stress fractures can occur spontaneously. Such injuries are most likely to happen when a horse is exhausted, and stress fractures are most likely when a horse is not thoroughly fit. Horses with head injuries (*see* Chapter 6) may be unconscious as a result of either concussion or coma.

Head Injuries
If the horse is in a coma (*see* Chapter 6), he will tend to lie still, on his side; he will be unresponsive, and usually have no ocular (eye) reflexes. If the corner of the eye is touched, the horse should blink (the palpebral reflex); absence of this blink reflex indicates that the horse is unconscious. If the surface of the eye is touched and no blinking results (the corneal reflex), brain death is indicated. In addition, stimuli such as probing of the nasal mucosa, or pouring water into the ear (these tests are best left to your veterinary surgeon) would elicit no response if no brain activity was present.

What to do if your horse has collapsed or can't rise

1. Call the vet.

2. Prevent further injury where possible and necessary: either prevent attempts to stand by applying weight to the neck, or aid standing.

3. Assess level of consciousness: is he awake and responsive?

   If he is unconscious, does he have any reflexes?

   If he can stand, can he balance normally? Is he in shock?

4. Institute any first-aid that is necessary (e.g. applying pressure to bleeding wounds), and keep him warm.

5. Whilst awaiting the vet, regularly (every five minutes) assess and record his level of consciousness, demeanour, heart rate, breathing rate, mucous-membrane colour, and circulation.

If he is merely concussed, a horse will respond to these stimuli, and blink when the ocular reflexes are tested. Some forms of brain damage can cause fitting, and bleeding from the ears and nose may also be seen.

Spine and Limb Injuries
Neck and back injuries (*see* Chapter 6) most commonly occur at the level of the base of the head, the lower neck, or the mid-lumbar area (*see* Figs 2–3). Such injuries can cause partial or complete paralysis of the limbs, which may not be accompanied by loss of consciousness. Horses with neck injuries may lie still in the position in which they fell, while those with back injuries may struggle to rise but be unsuccessful.

Similarly, horses with severe leg injuries may make recurrent attempts to rise, only to collapse again as they try to bear weight on the affected limb. On the other hand, a horse may simply be winded by a fall, and may lie still for a time, limbs unmoving, without having suffered any serious injury.

Horses with fractures of the limbs or spine may be unable to or may only be able to stand on three legs. In many cases, a fractured limb is found to be one on the underside as the horse lies, and it can be difficult to examine it properly, or even to realize that a fracture is present, without attempting to move the horse.

Winding

Horses that appear to have no serious injuries may be winded. They may be assisted to rise when they have got their breath back. The breathing rate should be monitored, and once the breathing rate is less than 30 breaths per minute, standing can be encouraged. This can be achieved by rolling the affected horse onto his brisket and, with one person steadying the head, and the other the tail, encouraging and steadying attempts to rise.

Exhaustion

Horses that collapse from exhaustion may simply be too unfit for their level of work, or they may be suffering from heatstroke or from some other underlying condition such as heart or respiratory disease.

Heatstroke
Heatstroke can easily occur when working an unfit horse on a hot day. Excessive sweating causes the horse to become dehydrated, which in turn decreases the amount of heat that can be lost by sweating. Affected horses tend to have an increased heart and respiratory rate, a weak or 'thready' pulse, and an elevated rectal temperature. This condition can be life-threatening, and the first priority is to cool the horse. This can be done by pouring cold water over his back to aid heat loss. Small amounts of water can also be offered to the horse to drink. Electrolytes and even intravenous fluids may also be necessary.

Thumps
Exhausted horses may suffer from electrolyte imbalances so severe that 'thumps' or 'synchronous diaphragmatic flutter'

Emergency treatment of injured recumbent horses

In any of the cases described, immediate veterinary attention should be sought. In the meantime, a basic examination may be carried out (*see* Chapter 2), and the heart and respiratory rates can be assessed. If, however, to examine the horse would be to endanger people (for example if the horse is fitting) then he should simply be kept as quiet as possible until the vet arrives. Reducing stimulation from light and noise can help diminish the severity of fits.

Where possible, tack may be loosened or removed, although obviously a bridle or headcollar should be retained to maintain control of the horse's head. Where possible, horses that are clearly unable to rise successfully but continue to try to do so should be prevented from further attempts to stand by having someone kneeling on their head or neck. Horses that are making no attempts to rise should be allowed to lie still; encouraging them to rise when the full extent of their injuries is unknown is not advisable. If they are encouraged to rise when they are not ready to do so, further damage to an injured area can occur, causing increased pain, and the horse may even sustain pelvic or limb fractures as he falls back to the ground.

results. This condition occurs through loss of calcium from the system, which in turn causes excitability of the phrenic nerve, which stimulates the diaphragm. The result is that the diaphragm begins to twitch in rhythm with the beats of the heart, and a loud 'thump' may be heard with each twitch, and a contraction seen in the muscles at the back of the chest. Calcium may have to be given intravenously.

These horses should be allowed to remain recumbent until they are ready to try to rise. They can then be assisted by a person steadying each end. Transportation should then be avoided for up to 48 hours to prevent further stress to the system occurring.

Conditions of this type can be avoided by ensuring that horses are healthy and are fit enough for the work that is asked of them. In addition, sufficient water and electrolytes should be given to horses working in hot weather.

Tying Up

Exertional rhabdomyolysis, or azoturia, commonly known as 'tying up', is a relatively common cause of symptoms ranging from poor performance, through lameness, to collapse. It affects the hindquarters in particular, where muscle spasm and associated damage results in pain and difficulty in moving. In addition, muscle-breakdown products enter the bloodstream and are filtered out by the kidneys. This results in a characteristic red-brown coloration of the urine, and can, in extremely severe cases, cause kidney damage and even death.

Symptoms usually occur soon after exercise is commenced, and can include progressive stiffening of the gait, difficulty moving the hind limbs and pelvis, signs of colic, resentment of palpation of the hindquarters (the muscles of which may

even feel swollen), and less specific signs relating to pain including increased temperature, distress, and increased pulse and respiration rates. Collapse and even death can result in severe cases.

An affected horse should immediately be rested, even if this means sending for a box or trailer to collect him and bring him back to a suitable place for treatment. Whilst the vet is awaited he should be kept warm, his temperature, pulse and respiration rates should be monitored, and he should be encouraged to drink.

As well as rest and fluids (maintaining hydration to protect the kidney is extremely important, and may necessitate the horse going on a drip), anti-inflammatory painkillers may be needed for treatment. Sedatives and tranquillizers are also sometimes used. Blood tests may be needed for a definite diagnosis to be made, although clinical signs are usually sufficient. Blood analysis is helpful in the assessment of the severity of an attack. Rest is advisable for at least one to two weeks, or until muscle enzyme levels in the blood are back to normal. Any further transportation should be delayed.

There are a number of different theories on what causes azoturia. Certain horses do appear to be particularly at risk, and there seems to be a hereditary predisposition. You can help to prevent attacks from occurring by feeding a well-balanced diet, by providing adequate electrolytes, and by implementing carefully planned exercise programmes. In addition, food rations should be cut back on rest days, and long periods of stabling should be avoided.

Cardiovascular Disease

Cardiovascular (heart) disease may cause collapse if the blood supply to the tissues is suddenly interrupted. In many cases, however, heart disease develops more gradually and causes more subtle symptoms.

The system of the heart and blood vessels carries oxygen to the tissues. The timing of the heart beats are regulated by a natural pacemaker within the heart muscle. Each time the heart beats, it squeezes out most of the blood within. Blood is forced out of the heart in a forward direction into the arteries by the closure of valves as the heart contracts, preventing backward flow. If the valves do not close fully, or the natural pacemaker does not beat regularly, the blood supply to the tissues is reduced. This can cause symptoms ranging from breathlessness and decreased exercise tolerance to exhaustion and collapse.

Horses that have collapsed as a result of heart disease are likely to have poor circulation, which can be identified by the pallor and increased capillary refill time of the mucous membranes. In addition, horses with heart disease are usually breathless, may cough, and are usually found to have extremely high heart rates. Whilst the vet is awaited, the horse should be kept warm and as quiet as possible. The heart rate should be monitored and recorded every five to ten minutes.

The vet may be able to hear a murmur, or an abnormal heart rate or rhythm using a stethoscope. In addition, other tests ranging from ECG to ultrasonography of the heart may be indicated in order to discover the precise problem within the heart. Unfortunately most heart conditions are not treatable in the horse. One of the most catastrophic types of heart disease occurs when rupture of the chordae tendinae occurs. The chordae tendinae are the fibres that hold the heart valves in position. Horses that have slightly leaky valves (and thus a murmur) may be able to cope well with exercise, although it may cause excess strain to the chordae tendinae. Sudden exertion can then result in the rupture of these fibres, and this prevents the valve from functioning. Forward flow of blood from the heart is consequently suddenly reduced and, despite

the heart rate speeding up, oxygen delivery to the tissues is suddenly and catastrophically lost. Sudden collapse and even death can result. There is no treatment.

Collapse can also follow the loss of the normal rhythm of the heart. An example of a condition in which this happens is atrial fibrillation, which can occur suddenly in a horse that is working hard. The heart suddenly stops pumping properly because the natural pacemaker fails: it tries to pump too fast, and this prevents blood from filling the heart between beats, thus yielding poor blood flow.

Such adverse effects on the circulation can also occur through blood loss via open wounds. Such wounds can be treated – where possible and safe to do so – by the application of pressure, which may stop the bleeding. Internal bleeding, on the other hand, cannot be staunched, and can cause collapse and even death. Internal bleeding occurs when there is rupture of major blood vessels caused by the bursting of an aneurysm (which can be secondary to worm damage), or to the laceration of a blood vessel by a broken bone. This can occasionally occur when a fragment of a broken rib punctures a major blood vessel in the chest, or even punctures the heart. In such cases loss of blood from the mouth and nose may be seen. Pelvic fractures can cause damage to the branches of the femoral arteries, which can result in uncontrollable bleeding into the abdomen, and ultimately death. Such horses may take any length of time from a few minutes to half an hour to bleed to death, and their death cannot be prevented.

Failure of effective circulation, whether it is caused by a heart problem, or blood loss, tends to result in increased heart and respiratory rates, a weak pulse, pale mucous membranes, and generalized weakness. Such horses should be rested and kept as quiet as possible whilst awaiting the vet; where possible, any blood loss should be staunched by application of pressure to the affected area.

Anaphylaxis

Horses may undergo acute collapse if they are exposed to something that they are allergic to. Although in most cases allergies cause either respiratory disease (such as obstructive pulmonary disease), or skin disease (such as urticaria, or hives), collapse can also occur.

In most cases horses that collapse from anaphylaxis have a recent history of medication or exposure to unusual plants. The horse may previously have had a mild allergic response to a similar stimulus, or may have been exposed to the medication or the plant in the past with no previous problems. Obviously future exposure to the stimulus should be avoided.

Symptoms may include obstructive pulmonary disease and hives, but signs of shock are also prevalent. The horse may tremble, and breathe heavily with difficulty and with audible gurgling (this relates to the build-up of inflammatory fluid in the lungs and the windpipe). In addition, temperature, pulse and respiration rates may be increased, and the mucous membranes are usually pale, with poor circulation. It can be difficult to distinguish such symptoms from signs of pain but if not treated appropriately and intensively the horse can die. Treatment may include anti-inflammatory medication, drugs to help breathing, tranquillizers to reduce distress, and even adrenaline. Some horses sadly do not recover despite treatment.

MOVING A COLLAPSED HORSE

Although it is generally advisable to keep horses as still and quiet as possible whilst awaiting a vet, and moving horses that are recumbent is generally not advisable, there are some instances in which a horse may have to be moved. If a horse is stuck on a fence or in a ditch in such a position that his breathing is affected, it makes sense to try to move him. (A horse stuck in a ditch can potentially drown in even a small amount of water.) It is important to remember that horses breathe only through the nose – they cannot breathe through the mouth – so the nostrils must be free of water and obstructions for breathing to take place. If a horse has sustained serious injuries, but is nevertheless able to breathe, moving him may cause him more pain than keeping him as still as possible in the position in which he is trapped. Each situation is different, and requires individual assessment. In all cases, no attempts should be made to move a horse unless it is safe to do so. Human injury should always be avoided.

If a horse is stuck on a fence, it may be easier to partially dismantle the fence than to drag the horse off, and this may also cause the horse less pain and distress. It is important to be able to keep the horse as still and quiet as possible during this process, both to avoid injuring those people working on the fence, and to avoid further injury to the horse. If the fence cannot be dismantled, or if a horse is stuck in a ditch, it may be necessary to drag the horse free. In any such situation it is important to have a strong headcollar that will not tighten, and a leadrope to control the head movements of the horse. Padding should be placed behind the ears and down the cheeks to prevent the headcollar causing chafing or excessive pressure on the skin and underlying tissues and nerves. In the conscious horse, the safest places to apply further rope to aid moving or controlling the horse are over the withers, round the brisket, and round the breech area (*see* Fig. 28). A rope over the withers can be used to drag a horse

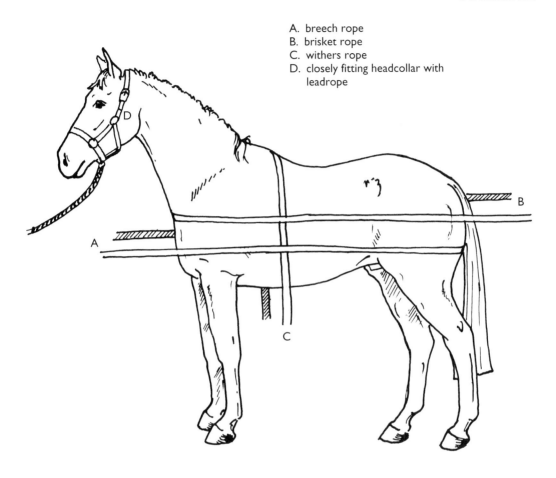

A. breech rope
B. brisket rope
C. withers rope
D. closely fitting headcollar with
   leadrope

Fig. 28 Managing the stuck, collapsed, or unconscious horse. Position the restraining ropes as shown. Wherever possible, the ropes, and the headcollar, should be padded to avoid causing damage through pressure or friction.

towards his feet, but can also be used to reduce struggling and to prevent rearing. A rope around the brisket or breech area can be used to drag the horse backwards or forwards. Such ropes should be well padded, and all knots used should be easily released and non-tightening. Where possible, mats or slings should be used to move the horse further, as soon as he is free enough of the object for them to be placed safely. Ropes around the legs should always be avoided in the conscious horse, as they may cause further injury or distress. An unconscious horse may be moved with the aid of well-padded ropes around his pasterns, but it must always be borne in mind that consciousness may be regained during such a process. Use of a blindfold in a conscious horse may aid control, and may reduce distress, although some horses do become more distressed when blindfolded.

6 Head, Neck and Spinal Trauma

HEAD INJURIES

If a horse has a head injury, the first priorioty is to assess whether or not there are signs of brain damage. In most cases, any bleeding or obvious fractures are of secondary significance to signs of brain injury. Brain damage can result from injuries that cause no external signs of damage, and is particularly likely to follow injuries to the back of the head. The horse that rears up and falls over backwards, or hits the back of his head, may well have more serious problems than the one that has been kicked in the face and has an unsightly wound.

Brain Injury

Initial symptoms consistent with damage to the brain include loss of consciousness, bleeding from head wounds, or from the ears or nose, and oozing of fluid from the ears or nose. Specific neurological (nerve-related) symptoms include loss of consciousness, inability to rise, incoordination, and loss of balance. These signs are usually at their worst immediately after the injury occurs, and they often improve with time. If neurological symptoms worsen while you are waiting for the vet, it is likely that further swelling or internal bleeding is placing more pressure on the brain and causing deterioration in the horse's condition. This is an extremely worrying sign,

and indicates the necessity for immediate and intensive treatment if the horse is to have a chance of survival.

In the short term, shock can mimic signs of serious brain injury by making animals apparently unaware of their surroundings. However, injuries that affect the brain and cause neurological symptoms usually involve concussion, bleeding or swelling, or skull fractures if they exert pressure on the brain.

If the horse does survive the short-term effects of such injuries, there may be long-term effects from brain damage. These can include difficulty in balancing (see Fig. 29), incoordination, and the development of epilepsy, and they may well prevent the horse from having a future. In addition, bone callus formation during the healing phase of fractures can continue to exert pressure on the brain; this can be progressive and untreatable, and cause further deterioration in neurological status.

Assessment of Serious Head Injuries

Whether or not the horse is standing is immediately obvious. If a horse is down but is conscious (see Chapter 5), it is important to let him take his own time to try to stand. Do not try to get him up as he may have other injuries that may be made worse by attempts to stand. Instead, after

64

Fig. 29 Loss of balance following brain injury.

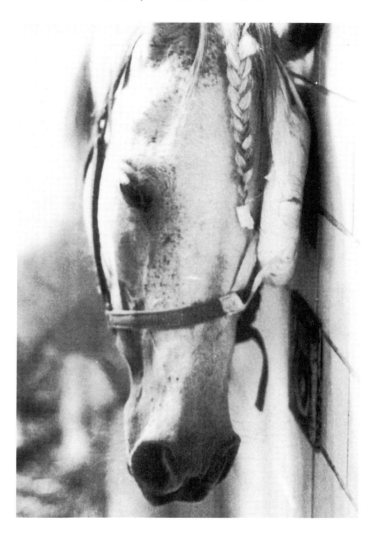

calling a vet, the first thing to do is to assess his mental state:

1. Check whether or not he is fully conscious and aware of his surroundings. This is usually immediately obvious.
2. If he is not, check that his heart is beating by feeling the chest behind the left elbow, or feeling for a pulse in the mandibular artery (*see* Chapter 2).
3. Check that he is breathing, and that his breathing is regular.

4. Then check that his brain is functioning by evaluating his palpebral and corneal reflexes.

The Palpebral and Corneal Reflexes
The palpebral reflex is the one that causes an animal to blink when you touch the inside corner of his eyelids. This reflex is normally present in conscious animals, although damage to the eyelid area may interfere with it. However, if the palpebral

reflex is not present, the horse is likely to be unconscious.

Checking the corneal reflex allows you to assess whether or not any brain activity is present. If the surface of the eye is touched, the horse should blink. Loss of the corneal reflex is an indicator of death of the brain.

Presence of the corneal but not the palpebral reflex suggests that the horse is alive but unconscious. Horses in this state may appear to be unaware of their surroundings but usually show responses to stimuli such as probing of the nasal mucosa, or applying water to the inside of the ear. These tests should not be undertaken without a vet present.

Horses that are concussed may suffer a brief loss of consciousness, while those with a more serious brain injury can remain unconscious for longer periods of time.

Initial assessment of the horse with suspected head injuries

1. Physical state: is he down?

2. Mental state: is he conscious (does he have a palpebral reflex) or unconscious? Or is he having seizures?

3. Brain functioning: does he have a corneal reflex?

First Aid

The Unconscious Horse
If a horse is alive but not conscious, emergency veterinary attention is obviously necessary. In the meantime the horse should not be moved, unless his posture is affecting his breathing, in which case the head should be moved gently to straighten the neck and throat to aid breathing. A rug may be placed over the horse to keep him warm. A horse that is fitting, or showing any signs of seizures, should be handled as little as possible, both to avoid exciting him further, and to avoid human injury. Covering the eyes and ears can help to reduce stimulation. The presence of seizure activity or fitting in horses with head injuries is often a poor sign; and where this behaviour cannot be controlled with medication, euthanasia may be the only option.

Whilst awaiting the vet, a basic first aid examination may be carried out (*see* Chapter 2), which should include measurement of the heart rate, the breathing rate and the temperature. In addition, pressure should be applied to any wounds that are bleeding (if this is possible), and the horse's mental state should be monitored.

The Down, Conscious Horse
Horses that are conscious but not standing should be allowed to continue lying down whilst the vet is awaited. In the meantime the heart rate and breathing rate can be monitored, a first-aid examination (*see* Chapter 2) performed, and appropriate first-aid treatment carried out.

The heart and breathing rates are usually increased if the horse is suffering pain, although they may be slowed or laboured owing to the presence of other injuries. It is a good idea to assess the horse's response to sounds and to touch, and to evaluate whether or not his posture is normal: horses that are conscious, and have no serious injuries, will manoeuvre themselves to lie on the brisket, and should hold their heads straight and not overly tilted to one side. All of this information may be of use to the vet when he arrives.

Unfortunately, experience shows us that horses that are recumbent for more than four hours – even if they are conscious and appear to have no serious injuries – rarely recover. In most cases, horses that do recover will have made successful attempts to stand within one or two hours of the injury.

The Standing, Conscious Horse

A horse that is standing should be kept as quiet as possible whilst awaiting the vet. If he is intent on standing but having difficulty balancing he may be helped to stand and then balanced by handlers positioned at the head and tail, or by manoeuvring him to a wall against which he can lean.

Horses that are not keen to stand should be encouraged to stay in a lying position while the vet is awaited, particularly if the angle of the head or neck, or the presence of abnormal eye position, suggest that a balance problem is present. In the meantime, preliminary examination and appropriate first-aid (*see* Chapter 4) can be carried out to assist the vet, as long as this does not distress the horse further.

Veterinary Assessment and Treatment

The vet will carry out a neurological examination to assess the nervous status of the patient. Where appropriate, and depending on the severity of the clinical signs, he may initiate treatment with anti-inflammatory agents (including steroids), diuretics (to reduce pressure on the brain), pain-relieving medication, antibiotics, and anti-tetanus medication.

NECK AND SPINAL INJURIES

Injuries to the spine in the neck and back are not uncommon in horses. In adult horses, the caudal cervical region (lower neck) and withers are common sites for injury caused when falling over, or running into jumps. As with injuries affecting the back of the head, neck trauma can also occur when a horse rears and falls over backwards. Young horses may also suffer upper neck fractures when pulling back whilst tied up, and horses of any age can

---

Neurological assessment

Neurological assessment includes the following tests:

1. Checking the palpebral and corneal reflexes (*see* page 65).

2. Checking vision (where eyes are not damaged) by use of the Menace test, which involves feinting a finger at the eye without touching any of the eyelashes or the eye itself; this normally causes a blink reflex. The pupillary-light reflex can also be used to test vision: this involves shining a bright light in each eye when in shadow, and watching for constriction of the pupil.

3. Checking that the eyes are moving normally within the orbit as the head moves. Eyes flicking fast from side to side (nystagmus) can be a sign of brain injury.

4. Checking response to sounds.

5. Checking that the skin twitches and the horse reacts in response to touch on the facial area. Also checking that the face is symmetrical (that one side is not drooping).

6. Checking that the horse can swallow normally, and that the larynx is moving normally.

7. Checking that the nerves to the body are working. This is done with the Panniculus test, which involves running a pen, or other pointed object, down each side of the spine and watching to see that the skin beneath it twitches, and the back dips. Anal tone and tail tone can also be assessed (is the anus slack? Is the tail floppy?).

8. In the walking horse, balance, coordination, gait, and placing reflexes (those that show that the horse knows where his feet are) can be checked.

receive neck and spinal injuries when they run into fences. Poll injuries can easily occur when horses rear up and hit the back of their heads, for instance in the stable or when being loaded in to a box. In addition, foals sometimes suffer from growth-plate fractures in the thoracic and lumbar spine (from the withers to the rump); because of the fragility of the bone in these areas in immature animals, this type of fracture can follow even apparently mild falls.

Symptoms of Spinal Injury

The clinical signs of spinal injury vary from severe paralysis to varying degrees of ataxia (incoordination) and weakness. These symptoms may be temporary, or they may be incurable. The affected horse may be seen to stumble, or to have difficulty negotiating obstacles on the ground. If the area of damage is in the neck, it is likely that the gait of all four limbs will be affected; if the injury is behind the withers (i.e. behind the point at which the nerves to the forelimbs leave the spine), only the hind limbs may be affected.

Symptoms of incoordination and weakness are usually worsened by asking the horse to perform more complex movements such as circling, backing, or walking over obstacles. Other tests include pulling the tail to either side as the horse walks to check that the horse can resist the pull and walk straight as a normal horse would, and pushing the horse to the side from the shoulder to similarly test his balance.

Symptoms of Neck Injury

In the worst scenario, injuries to the upper neck can (in much the same way as head injuries) cause death or complete paralysis if the spinal cord becomes damaged. This can occur at the time of the injury, or signs may become apparent over subsequent hours as swelling develops in the area of the injury or movement of bony fragments occurs as the horse moves or struggles. Lesser injuries can cause signs including partial paralysis or ataxia (lack of coordination) and, of course, neck pain and stiffness.

If any of these signs are seen, veterinary attention should be sought, and in the meantime the horse should be kept as quiet and still as possible. Confirmation of the presence or absence of a fracture cannot be made without further investigation of the area, and this usually requires transporting the horse (which is contraindicated in the immediate post-injury period). The long-term prognosis is difficult to assess at this stage; instead, the horse should be managed with box-rest and anti-inflammatory medication, and regularly reassessed. In the recovery period there is usually little else that can be done; but feeding and watering the horse at head level is to be recommended.

Less serious injuries in the neck include ligamentar and muscular strains. The symptoms that such injuries cause can be so subtle as to remain unrecognized for some time. These symptoms may include stiffness, inability to flex and accept the bit, and difficulty in bending and in working on both diagonals. Muscular asymmetry may also be seen. Those cases that are severe enough to cause forelimb lameness or unlevelness are usually more easily recognizable.

Initial Treatment of Neck Injuries
Treatment includes the use of cool-packs to reduce swelling and inflammation, as well as anti-inflammatory medication prescribed by your vet. In addition, in some cases a consultation with an equine physiotherapist can be useful because various exercises can help to aid mobilization of all the structures after the acute

inflammatory phase of the injury. These exercises include encouraging your horse to bend his neck to both sides and down, by offering him food from the area of his elbows or from between his front legs. This can be repeated several times each day and will encourage him to bend within the limits of what is comfortable for him. These limits are then gradually stretched as he becomes more mobile. Once his mobility has been improved at rest, work can be done under saddle to encourage him to bend equally in both directions; this will necessarily include neck mobility as well as back mobility.

Injuries of the Withers

Fractures of the withers can cause acute bilateral forelimb lameness. They are usually easily recognized by the abnormal contour of the area and localization of pain in this area. The diagnosis can be confirmed by X-ray, but this may be delayed where transporting the horse is contra-indicated. Most cases heal with box-rest alone, and many of these horses eventually return to full work, although they are likely to need their saddles refitted and stuffed to fit them individually as they may well develop asymmetries in the wither area.

Less serious injuries to the withers can occur either as a result of muscular or ligamentar strains, or as a result of poor saddle fit. Low-grade forelimb lameness may be seen, or the horse may simply appear to be stiff or pottery. These horses often move at their worst when under saddle, and in many cases are cold backed when saddled, or resent saddling and girthing. Palpation of the bony surface of the top of the withers, and of the muscles on either side, may elicit pain or muscle spasm. Standing the horse square and then viewing the withers from the rear, over the rump, often allows asymmetries to be recognized (see Fig. 30). Sometimes such asymmetries can most easily be appreciated by standing under the horse's neck, facing his rear, and feeling both sides of the withers at the same time.

If a withers problem is suspected, the saddle fit should be assessed. Even if the saddle fit is good, extra padding may be needed once riding is resumed. Rest is obviously important, anti-inflammatory packing and/or medication may be necessary (see above), and certain exercises can be helpful to aid mobilization of the area. These include those mentioned above to help mobilization of the neck, as well as gentle stretching exercises, including pulling the forelimbs forward from the knee, as one would after saddling to stop the girth pinching, and pulling the leg back in a similar manner.

Back Injuries

Back injuries are extremely common in the ridden horse. They commonly involve the muscles and ligaments of the spine, and are usually associated with poor conformation, poor saddle fit, and poor seating on the part of the rider. Badly fitting saddles and poor riding can be improved. Conformation cannot, and it's important to be aware that the horse with a particularly long back or dipped back may not be as strong in this area as one with better conformation. Equally, a horse with a particularly short back may be more likely to develop back pain caused when adjacent dorsal spinous processes impinge upon one another (so called 'kissing' spines). Traumatic injuries may also be involved, and commonly follow falls or sliding stops. Occasionally, traumatic injuries involve the vertebrae and spinal cord. Back pain can also occur when pain in a limb causes a horse to move abnormally (see Chapter 11).

Fractures of the back can be catastrophic, although some do heal. Where

69

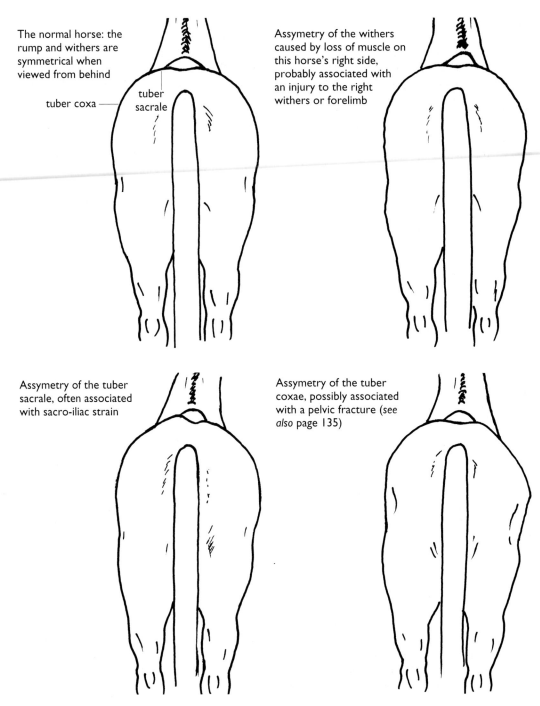

The normal horse: the rump and withers are symmetrical when viewed from behind

tuber coxa

tuber sacrale

Assymetry of the withers caused by loss of muscle on this horse's right side, probably associated with an injury to the right withers or forelimb

Assymetry of the tuber sacrale, often associated with sacro-iliac strain

Assymetry of the tuber coxae, possibly associated with a pelvic fracture (see also page 135)

Fig. 30 *Effects on the back from injury to the withers, sacro-iliac joint, or pelvis.*

they do not involve the spinal cord, they may ultimately allow the horse to regain his performance ability. However, in many cases they result in the horse being unable to carry a rider. After the initial healing phase, during which the horse is box-rested, gentle exercise and physiotherapy are to be recommended to allow mobilization of the affected area. Spinal fractures involving the spinal cord cause partial or complete paralysis, and sadly are likely to necessitate euthanasia (*see* Chapter 5).

Less serious injuries of the back are extremely common. Affected horses may show very subtle symptoms such as poor impulsion, loss of 'spark', decreased tolerance of exercise, resentment of stroking or grooming, difficulty jumping, and failure to track up properly and unite in canter. Horses with sore backs are also often cold-backed to saddle, may resent saddling and girthing, and may be inclined to buck in attempts to remove their rider. At exercise these horses may appear lame, particularly in the hind limbs, or may simply not move freely.

Veterinary Examination
Examination of the horse with an injured back includes careful observation of the back for symmetry, and palpation. Palpation of the back, both by running the fingers down the spinous processes, and by feeling the muscles on either sides of the back, may elicit pain or muscle spasm. The mobility of the back can be assessed by running a ticklish object such as a ballpoint pen along either side of the spine. A normal horse will dip away as the pen passes over the saddle area, and will then arch his back up as the pen passes over the rump. In addition, pinching the underside of the chest will normally induce arching upwards of the back. A horse with severe muscle spasm will be unable to move his back freely in this manner.

When moving, the horse with a sore back may be lame, or may simply appear stiff. On a circle he will usually be unable to bend, and when ridden may be unable to drop his head and accept the bit. When turned tightly he may have difficulty balancing, and may be unable to cross his hind legs normally. He may also have difficulty backing up.

Further diagnostic techniques that can be useful include blood tests to screen for signs of muscle damage, X-rays, ultrasound scanning of the back muscles, and nuclear scintigraphy.

Initial treatment of back problems

For most mild back problems, rest is the most important treatment. In addition, anti-inflammatory packs and medication are usually required, and stretching exercises and gentle tail traction can be helpful. In many cases your vet may recommend some physiotherapy treatment. Once the horse is past the initial stages of the problem, a slowly ascending exercise programme will be needed. Warming the horse up by lungeing him before he is tacked up and before he is mounted may also be helpful. Working the horse in both directions to encourage bending, and equally on both diagonals at trot and canter, can help to keep the back supple and mobile. After any kind of back injury, changes in the contour of the saddle area may well necessitate refitting of the saddle.

The Sacro-iliac Joint
The sacro-iliac joint attaches the pelvis (and thus the hind limbs) to the spine. This joint is normally relatively immobile, but the ligament that holds it together can become strained as a result of trauma, commonly following a sliding stop or a fall. This can cause hind-limb lameness or foot dragging, poor propulsion, and failure to track up properly. In addition, looking at the horse carefully from behind when

he is standing square on a level surface may allow asymmetry of the tuber sacrale to be seen (*see* Fig. 30). As the horse moves away the tuber sacrale may be seen to move relative to the spine, which is not normal. On feeling the rump, pressure on the bones of the pelvis may elicit pain.

This condition may be overdiagnosed, particularly by non-veterinary practitioners. Accurate diagnosis may necessitate investigation at a referral centre, which will include nuclear scintigraphy. With appropriate treatment – which usually means box-rest followed by a controlled exercise programme to build up supporting muscle in the area – some affected horses recover from the condition. Horses that have injured the sacro-iliac joint may always have a slight lack of symmetry in this area.

Pelvic Injury

Pelvic fractures, and other types of pelvic injury, can cause asymmetry of the muscles of the rump (*see* Figs 3 and 57), and hind-limb lameness or stiffness. Treatment usually involves rest and anti-inflammatory medication, although some pelvic fractures do need surgical correction. Pelvic injuries are discussed more fully in Chapter 11.

Back practitioners

In all cases where back and neck injuries of any type occur, veterinary assessment is to be recommended, if only to rule out the presence of fractures, and to prescribe effective anti-inflammatory and painkilling medication. Veterinary examination should precede the attention of chiropractors, osteopaths, physiotherapists, and other back practitioners. That way your vet can investigate the problem fully, and treat it appropriately as promptly as possible. Physiotherapy, where necessary, can be carried out far more successfully in conjunction with attention to any other problems that are present.

Some back practitioners are extremely knowledgeable and obtain very good results. However, many have no formal training and little knowledge of anatomy. Inappropriate use of manipulative techniques can, on rare occasions – such as in horses with undiagnosed cracks or fractures of the bones of the spine – have catastrophic results. The safest way of choosing someone to assess your horse's back is to consult your vet, who is likely to know of reputable local practitioners. It is advisable to use a qualified equine chartered physiotherapist, since they are trained in equine anatomy and can use and prescribe safe exercises for your horse as well as faradism, heat treatment, therapeutic ultrasound, and laser therapy in cases where these are appropriate. There are, undoubtedly, some people with no formal training who work on horses' backs with good results, and discussion with other horse owners will allow you to identify which of them have the best reputations; but care is to be advised in the choice of those who are unqualified.

---

7 Face and Eye Injuries

Although they are relatively rare, head injuries in horses should always be assessed as soon as possible because of their potential for involving underlying structures, and for having serious consequences. In most cases head injuries appear to be more serious than they actually are; but in some that appear innocuous, serious problems can develop. For this reason all horses with head injuries should be examined as soon as possible by a vet.

In most cases head injuries occur in the field as a result of a kick, or of running into fences, but they can also be sustained whilst exercising or competing: from

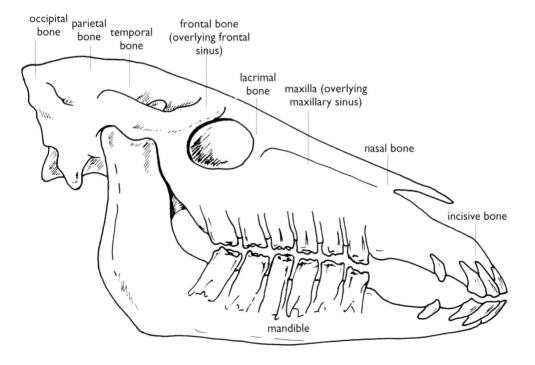

occipital bone
parietal bone
temporal bone
frontal bone (overlying frontal sinus)
lacrimal bone
maxilla (overlying maxillary sinus)
nasal bone
incisive bone
mandible

Fig. 31 The skeletal anatomy (bones) of the head.

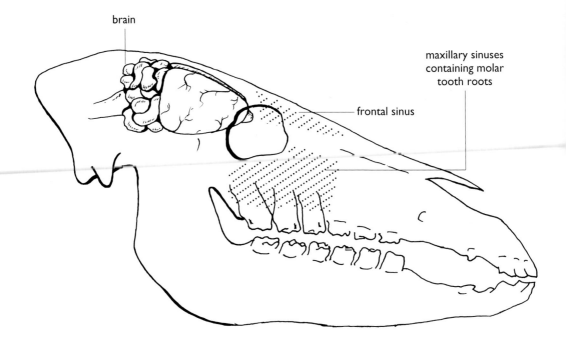

Fig. 32 *The position of the brain and the sinuses in the head at the midline.*

running into jumps, from tripping or falling over jumps, from rearing and falling over backwards, or from otherwise colliding with solid objects such as polo mallets or balls.

Most commonly, head injuries involve simple abrasions or wounds (*see* Chapter 8), but in some cases deeper structures are involved. These include the bones of the skull and jaws (*see* Fig. 31), the sinuses, the teeth, the eyes, and the ears. Severe injuries can even involve damage of the deeper skull bones that form the covering of the brain (*see* Fig. 32). These cases need to be identified quickly as they may necessitate emergency attention, particularly if the brain might be involved. Since the brain is involved in the control of involuntary as well as voluntary movements, damage to the brain can manifest itself in a number of ways (*see* Chapter 5).

EYE INJURIES

Whenever head injuries occur, the possibility of associated damage to the eyes should be considered. The eyes are very fragile organs and are easily damaged. Although the eyelids provide the eyes with some protection, eye injuries are still common. In some cases, for instance those in which there is swelling or visible damage to the ocular structures, it is immediately obvious that an eye injury has occurred. However, some ocular injuries are not visible in the early stages, and others, despite their initially mild or innocuous appearance, may still have the potential ultimately to cause the loss of an eye. For this reason, whenever an ocular injury is suspected, veterinary attention should be sought promptly.

Symptoms that indicate that an eye has become injured include discomfort, swelling of the area, closing of the eye, over-production of tears and weeping, redness of the ocular membranes, and obvious signs of injury such as discharges, bleeding, and lacerations and marks on the surface of the eye.

The structure of the eye (*see* Fig. 33) is such that most forms of direct trauma involve damage to the cornea (the front surface of the eye) and, in some cases, penetration of deeper tissues. Other forms of trauma, such as that resulting from high-speed impact, and damage to the tissues surrounding the eye, can result in injury to the deeper structures, such as the lens or optic nerve, without necessarily involving severe corneal damage. An assessment of the injuries needs to be made at an early stage, as prompt treatment gives the best chance of healing.

Examination of the Eye

Examination of the eye requires a systematic approach. It is also important to be aware that the horse may not be able to see from the affected eye so he should be approached with special gentleness and care. First the eyes and the surrounding area on the face are assessed for symmetry and signs of obvious swelling. The area around the eye should be felt, and any signs of bony instability that might indicate the presence of fractured bone should be noted. If the eye is closed, the lids can be gently parted, and the eye itself examined. In some cases the eye or surrounding membranes may be particularly painful or inflamed, and it may not be possible to open the eye without first sedating and/or anaesthetizing the horse.

Any signs of discharge from the eye itself or from the corner of the eyelids

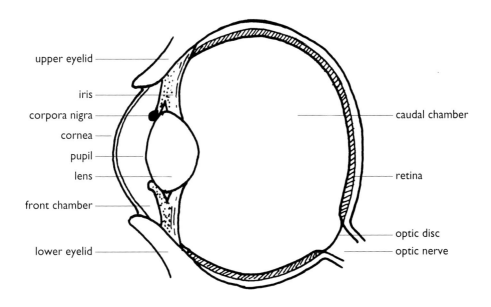

Fig. 33 The structure of the horse's eye in cross-section.

upper eyelid

iris

corpora nigra

cornea

pupil

lens

front chamber

lower eyelid

caudal chamber

retina

optic disc

optic nerve

should be noted, and if the eye can be examined, the sizes of the pupils should be compared. Severe injuries such as rupture of the eye itself (in which it may be seen to be collapsed, and oozing matter from within) or prolapse of the eye (in which the eye is no longer situated within its eyelids) warrant urgent attention. First aid is inappropriate in such cases. The horse should merely be kept as quiet as possible, preferably in a darkened box, until the vet arrives. In less serious cases, there is little that can be done in terms of first aid, but any discharges may be wiped away with cotton wool soaked in clean water. In all cases veterinary attention should be sought.

Veterinary examination usually includes the examination of the structures of the eye using an opthalmoscope. (The exception is those cases in which the damage to the eye is so serious that this is not necessary, i.e. when the globe is ruptured or prolapsed.) The eye must be examined thoroughly, and this may necessitate sedation or anaesthesia. The corneal surface, anterior chamber of the eye, iris and pupil, lens, posterior chamber of the eye, and retina are all investigated, and any signs of abnormality are noted. In addition, the whole area should be examined carefully to check that there are no foreign bodies present. Small pieces of straw or twigs are commonly found in horses' eyes and can cause serious damage if they are not removed carefully and promptly.

In some cases a corneal ulcer can be seen straight away as a shallow, whitish hollow on the surface of the eye. In addition, blood vessels may be seen running across the surface of the eye during the healing process. In other cases, it is necessary to use a fluorescent dye to show up the ulcer. The dye is taken up by damaged areas and so shows the extent of any ulceration.

Tears drain from the corner of the eye, via the naso-lacrimal duct, to the nose, and so traces of the dye should appear in the nostril after its application to the eye. The absence of dye at the nostril indicates blockage or damage of the naso-lacrimal duct. In addition to showing up any corneal injuries, fluorescent dye can be used to monitor the healing process.

Sometimes inflammation of the front chamber of the eye – a secondary effect of a long-standing ulcer of this type – can cause the whole of the eye to take on a pearly, bluish-white appearance. This can also cause fixing of the pupil so that it can no longer respond normally to light, which can lead to serious problems with vision. Infection of the eye can produce the appearance of pus within the eye, and trauma can produce blood. Whilst all ocular injuries need prompt treatment in order to prevent loss of vision, injuries of this nature are particularly serious.

Treatment

Treatment of ocular injuries will vary according to the damage involved. Any injuries that include rupture or prolapse of the globe require urgent surgery, under general anaesthesia, which may involve the loss of the affected eye. Orbital fractures may also require surgical correction.

Lacerations of the eyelids are not uncommon, and must receive urgent veterinary attention because they usually need to be stitched. The perfect realignment of the eyelid edges, in such cases, is of paramount importance since rough edges can cause future damage to the cornea. Similarly, lacerations of the third eyelid of conjunctival membranes need to be carefully treated, though most do not need surgery.

Treatment of corneal injuries and ulcers depends on their depth. Superficial injuries usually heal with medical treatment alone; deeper injuries may require surgery. Deep and severe ulceration can cause temporary or permanent loss of transparency of the surface of the eye, and fixing of the pupil, as a result of inflammation. The use of anti-inflammatory medication and the regular use of atropine drops (which cause dilation of the pupil) to keep the pupil mobile may therefore be required.

In the autumn and winter months, mild ocular inflammation with no underlying disease can sometimes occur from irritation caused by wind and rain. This results in a watery ocular discharge that may occur with or without significant conjunctivitis (inflammation of the membranes around the eye), and usually requires treatment with eye ointments.

Most ocular injures require medical treatment with antibiotics, which can be given systemically, or may be applied to the area in the form of ointment or drops (see Appendix, Fig. 74 for details of how to apply ocular medication). Anti-inflammatory medication may also be used, but those anti-inflammatories that contain steroids should be avoided where possible, since they may suppress healing. Most injuries involving the tissues around the eye, and most shallow corneal injuries, heal with no long-term ill effect. Deeper corneal injuries may cause areas of corneal scarring, which if minor may cause no visual problems; more extensive scarring can result in partial or complete loss of vision. Severe injuries can ultimately result in shrinkage of the globe of the eye (the *pthisis bulbi*) which can cause loss of vision.

FACIAL WOUNDS

Wounds on the face (*see also* Chapter 8) that penetrate the full thickness of the skin may need to be sutured, and certainly need to be carefully washed out so that bacteria are not forced deeper into the wound. There are many blood vessels, nerves, and other structures lying under the skin, so early assessment of such injuries is important so that your vet can assess the likelihood of any of these structures being involved.

Damage to the tear duct, for instance, can result in the tears no longer being able to drain efficiently into the nose, and this can cause swellings of the face, and tear-staining from tear overflow. Damage to salivary ducts can cause similar problems.

Nerve damage can cause permanent or temporary loss of mobility of the face. This is most commonly observed when the facial nerve is damaged in 'Horner's syndrome' (*see* Fig. 34). This nerve is involved in the normal movement of the ear, upper eyelid and lip, and its damage can result in drooping of the upper lip on the side of the damaged nerve, as well as drooling, drooping of the upper eyelid, and drooping of the ear. Although this condition is normally seen when the nerve is damaged by a wound, it can also occur through pressure from an over-tight headcollar.

The most mild types of head injury are bruises and grazes. They are commonly seen in horses with colic, who sustain self-inflicted facial abrasions in the course of lying down and rolling. Whilst grazes may cause swelling, and may look raw and painful, they are usually of no serious consequence unless they affect the eyes. Even superficial abrasions to the surface of the eyes can cause serious damage and, if not treated promptly, can result in partial or complete loss of vision.

Superficial abrasions to the face are, like similar injuries elsewhere, treated by gentle cleaning with a dilute antiseptic solution (*see* pages 88 and 89) applied with cotton wool. (For injuries close to the eye, plain water rather than antiseptic should be used.) Petroleum jelly may be used on the area surrounding the injury to prevent serum leakage (the fluid exuded by damaged tissues) from scalding the skin, and anti-inflammatory creams may be applied.

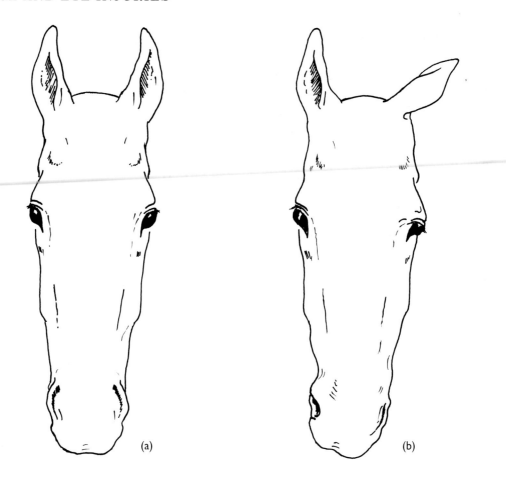

Fig. 34 Horner's syndrome: (a) The normal horse. (b) Damage to the left facial nerve – drooping of the ear, eyelid and lip on that side.

THE JAWS

Injuries from kicks, and other sources of trauma, can result in fractures of the jaw bones. These may cause few external signs, and in some cases horses may even continue to try to graze. Facial swelling is often seen, though, and the affected horse may bleed from the mouth. On opening the mouth, an obvious lack of symmetry of the jaws can usually be observed.

These fractures usually do well if prompt surgical treatment is implemented to stabilize the fracture, as long as the site of the fracture is not too near the angle of the jaw and the jaw joint. Teeth may be lost as a result of such injuries to the jaw, and future treatment is obviously likely to include regular dentistry to correct any tooth problems that may develop as a result of malalignment of the jaws.

THE LIPS AND TONGUE

Lip and tongue wounds are usually readily identified. Since the tongue is well supplied with blood vessels, tongue injuries cause copious bleeding. The tongue is a highly mobile organ and cannot be sutured under standing sedation, so, although minor injuries may heal with antibiotics and anti-tetanus medication alone, extensive wounds need to be sutured under general anaesthetic as soon as possible.

Lip and tongue injuries can be inflicted by the bit, either when a horse has been pulling against it, or when it is poorly fitting or sharp. These wounds usually heal well if the horse is rested, and bitting is not attempted until they are completely healed. (Of course, when the horse is ready to receive the bit again, you should be certain that you have remedied the cause of the original wound, which means ensuring that the bit is of good quality and properly fitted.)

Tongue injuries caused by the application of a twitch to the tongue are sometimes seen. Twitches should only ever be applied to the nose (see Fig. 18). Application of a twitch to the tongue is inhumane and causes serious damage by occluding the blood supply of this organ.

Lip and cheek injuries can also be caused by sharp teeth (see Fig. 35), so regular dental examinations (every six to twelve months) are extremely important. Signs of these injuries include difficulty and discomfort when eating, and resentment of the bit. Such wounds usually heal well with medical treatment as soon as the teeth have been attended to.

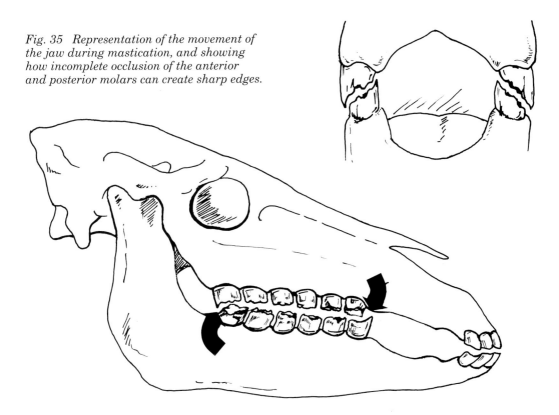

Fig. 35 Representation of the movement of the jaw during mastication, and showing how incomplete occlusion of the anterior and posterior molars can create sharp edges.

FACIAL FRACTURES

Injuries that involve fractures of the bones of the skull have the potential to prove extremely serious. However, in many cases the damage is limited to the area of the front of the face. Though these injuries can look extremely nasty in the short term, there may be no neurological effect (damage to the nerves or the brain). Injuries involving the back of the head may not appear to be particularly severe, but they are more likely to be associated with damage to the brain.

Kick injures are often responsible for damage to the face, and may cause depression fractures of the bones that overlie the sinuses, without damaging any structures associated with the brain (*see* Figs 31–32). If the skin is not broken, and as long as the bone fragments retain their blood supply, they may heal without surgical treatment. If fragments of bone do lose their blood supply, they die; this can set up a source of infection, and so they may need to be removed.

Although inappropriate management of small wounds associated with this type of fracture can result in sinus and even tooth-root infections, in most cases such skin wounds heal if managed correctly with prompt veterinary attention and antibiotic therapy. Grossly contaminated (dirty) and extensive wounds in this area should be surgically debrided (much of the damaged tissue may need to be scraped or cut away) so that infected pieces of tissue and bone fragments can be removed. Any fractures in this area can cause permanent loss of the normal facial contour, which, though it may be no problem for the horse, may not be aesthetically pleasing.

The Teeth

Cracked or split teeth can result from eating hard objects, but they may also be caused by more serious injuries. Damaged teeth are susceptible to root infections.

Symptoms of tooth injury include difficulty or discomfort when eating, quidding, and resentment of the bit. In many cases, few symptoms are seen because horses have little sensation in their teeth. However, if secondary root infection occurs, firm swellings may develop on the cheeks or under the lower jaw and cause discomfort. These swellings may also be painful to the touch. Some of the cheek teeth have their roots in the sinuses (*see* Fig. 32), and if these become infected a sinus infection can result and cause nasal discharges. If not treated appropriately at this stage, infection can spread into the jaw bone and cause osteomyelitis (inflammation and infection of the bone), which is a serious condition. In most cases teeth that are damaged and infected need to be surgically removed under a general anaesthetic by a vet.

Damage to the gums in immature horses can cause abnormal tooth growth, resulting in a tooth growing in an abnormal direction or in an abnormal position. In such cases tooth removal or regular dentistry is required as the aberrant tooth will not be ground down by the corresponding tooth in the opposing jaw.

In any cases where the teeth do not meet normally (whether through abnormal growth, or the removal of a tooth) regular dentistry (every six months) by an experienced vet or dentist is necessary to prevent teeth that are not being worn down from damaging the gums of the opposing jaw.

8 Skin Injuries ——————

WOUNDS

Avoiding Injury

Wounds are one of the commonest types of injury to the horse. Where possible, therefore, the avoidance of wounds is to be encouraged. Although the best standards of care and management can reduce the chance of wounds being sustained, these injuries still occur quite often.

Horses that are most likely to become wounded obviously include those whose work is dangerous. Wounds tend to occur during high-speed work or collision with obstacles, so racehorses, point-to-pointers, eventers, and showjumpers are all at risk, as are driving horses. Horses used for more controlled activities such as dressage and for hacking are less likely to sustain wounds whilst working. The use of appropriate boots and bandages for the work being undertaken is to be advised. Those individuals that tend to overreach should wear overreach boots, and brushing boots can be used to prevent injuries occurring when one leg strikes that on the other side, and to protect the cannon area in the event of a fall.

Ill-fitting boots or tack can just as easily cause injuries as prevent them. Abrasions and wounds can be caused by poorly fitting tack, as well as boots that are applied too loosely, too tightly, or left on too long. Bandages over wounds or injuries, particularly where they are being used in the long term, often cause abrasions. Pressure sores can result where bandages cover underlying structures, in particular those that protrude, such as the point of the elbow or hock, or the accessory carpal bone on the inside of the knee. For these reasons, bandages should be well padded, and where they cross such structures they should be applied in such a way as to avoid pressure. Poor fit of the bridle, saddle or girth can result in the development of galls. Poorly fitting or inappropriate bits, or damaged bits with rough edges, can cause lip and cheek injuries.

Protection of horses while travelling should include the use of rugs, and padded travelling boots to provide protection from the hock or knee down. Boxes and trailers should be well padded and well maintained, and nervous horses should be transported with a safe travelling companion. Floors and ramps should have non-slip surfaces, and if the gap between them at the hinge is wide it should be covered or filled during loading and unloading to prevent lower limbs becoming trapped.

In the stable and field, wounds can be avoided by ensuring that the environment is as safe as possible. Loose nails and broken planks should be dealt with quickly. Hay-racks and food and water bowls should not have sharp edges, and should be positioned appropriately (i.e. hay-racks should be high enough to avoid horses getting their feet stuck in them!). Horses can also get their feet stuck in haynets; the use of hay-bags may be preferable. In the field, post-and-rail fencing is less dangerous than wire, and barbed wire should never be used. Where wire fences are used they should be clearly marked so horses can see them, and an inner electric-tape fence should be added to prevent horses injuring themselves on the wire. Obstacles within the field should be removed or fenced off, and all fences should be checked regularly at least once a week. If horses are to be fed in the field, sufficient space should be given for all to gain access to food.

Horses tend to be most settled and happy if they are always turned out in the same groups. Injuries commonly follow the introduction of a new horse to a field. From a management point of view, therefore, horses should be allowed to become familiar with one another before being turned out together. If a new horse is to be introduced, horses should be led out and hand-grazed for a time before being released, or should initially be turned out in adjoining fields to allow them to become used to each other. Kick injuries commonly occur when mares are in season. Geldings and mares should therefore be turned out separately where possible, and double fencing between 'flirty' mares and 'riggy' geldings is to be advised. In most cases stallions should be turned out separately away from mares and geldings.

Assessment of Wounds

The initial assessment of skin wounds is of extreme importance because they are one of the most common injuries that affect horses, and their inappropriate treatment can sometimes lead to fatality. Those wounds that, for instance, bleed copiously, usually seem to be far more severe than the small puncture wounds, which more often have serious consequences. It is important to keep a clear head, and to assess a situation sensibly, so that emergency attention can be sought where

---

Is this an emergency?

• Is blood gushing or spurting from the wound?

• Is the horse unable to bear weight on the limb and/or are obvious fractures present?

If the answer to either of the above is yes, call a vet urgently. In the meantime institute first aid where appropriate (stem the bleeding if you can).

---

necessary, and appropriate first aid can be instituted where possible (*see* Chapter 4).

Is There Bleeding?

Bleeding from wounds generally appears to be more severe than it is. The average horse has approximately 50 pints (28.4 litres) of blood, and can lose up to 10 per cent (i.e. 5 pints/2.8 litres) of this with few ill effects. If, however, blood loss from wounds involving large blood vessels is not reduced or prevented, bleeding to death can occur in under half an hour. Luckily, though, most of the major blood vessels run internally and are unlikely to be damaged by injuries. The exceptions to these are the main blood vessels in the neck, and those running into the front and hind limbs. Damage to these can cause uncontrollable bleeding.

It is important to be able to distinguish between arterial and venous bleeding (*see* Chapter 3), because arterial injuries are usually more serious. Arteries are directly connected to the heart, and emit a spurt of blood in time with each heart beat. Veins, on the other hand, contain blood that is returning to the heart and is at lower pressure, and they tend to ooze blood (*see* Fig. 36). The blood from an artery is also a far brighter red than that from a vein because it contains more oxygen. Where severe bleeding (i.e. gushing or spurting of blood

The commonest injury involving serious blood loss is the wound in the pastern area that involves the palmar digital artery on either side of the back of the foot just above the bulbs of the heel. A horse is unlikely to bleed to death from such a wound, but copious bleeding can be seen and can be serious if not controlled by pressure bandaging whilst waiting for the vet.

Is There Bony Damage?
Wounds involving bone damage (*see* Chapter 11) may be apparent if there are fragments of bone within the skin deficit, but they may also be suspected in the presence

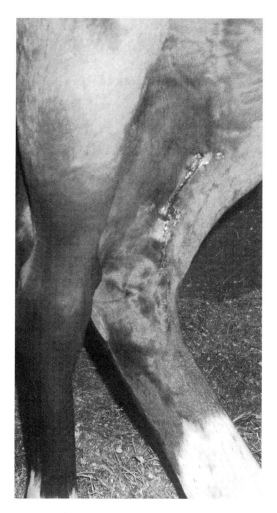

Fig. 36 Blood oozing from an injury to the inside of the thigh.

rather than oozing or dripping) is present, urgent veterinary attention should be sought, and in the meantime, where possible, the bleeding should be stopped. This can usually be achieved by the application of sufficient pressure. This can be achieved either by applying layers of tight bandages, or, where bandaging is not possible, by applying direct pressure with a hand-held dressing.

The characteristics of wounds

Pay attention to:

Discharges: Blood?
Serum?
Synovial fluid?
Pus?

Position: Proximity to joints or tendons?
High- or low-motion area (is it over a joint)?

Depth: Skin only?
Skin and underlying muscle?
Involvement of deeper structures – nerves, blood vessels, bones, etc.? (*See* Fig. 38.)

Extent: Simple (single) wound?
Multiple, with or without skin deficits?

Tetanus: Is the horse vaccinated against tetanus, and if so how recently?

All of this information will help you to decide how urgently the wound requires veterinary attention, and will be useful for the vet so that he knows exactly what equipment will be needed to deal with the wound.

of a wound on a limb on which the horse is unable to bear weight. Such wounds should not be handled, since attempts to provide pressure or support to fractured bones usually cause further pain and result either in human injury or in the horse being so distressed that he injures himself further. Instead, the horse should be kept as still and quiet as possible whilst urgent veterinary attention is awaited.

Where is the Wound?
In addition to noting the obvious symptoms, your assessment of a wound should take account of its position, and thus the likelihood of its involving deeper structures. This chapter explains the course of action for the treatment of shallow wounds, and also of deep wounds involving the muscles. The likely involvement of other deeper structures depends on the position of a wound, and what structures lie beneath. Such wounds are discussed in other chapters in more detail.

Is a Synovial Structure Involved?
While wounds involving fractured bones or excessive bleeding obviously require urgent veterinary attention, wounds involving synovial structures – such as joints and tendon sheaths – also require rapid attention. Although they might initially appear to be less serious, wounds involving the joints or tendon sheaths (*see* Fig. 37) can be dangerous because if they do not receive veterinary attention within four to six hours, irreversible infection can occur, and this can necessitate euthanasia.

In most cases of joint or tendon sheath damage, discharge of synovial fluid from the wound will be seen. Synovial fluid is normally a clear, yellowish colour and, when rubbed between finger and thumb, it feels slightly tacky. It is easy, however, to confuse this with serum – the clearish fluid released from blood as it clots — which can be released from any wound. Synovial fluid from injured joints tends to spurt out as the joint is moved and pressure is exerted on it. However, that from the tendon sheaths is

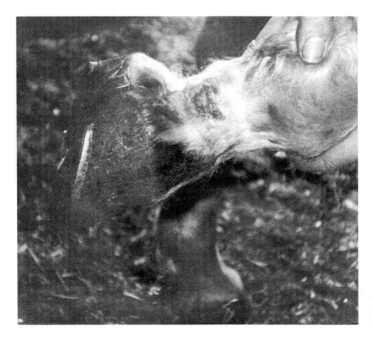

Fig. 37 This small wound to the back of the pastern involves the tendon sheath.

Fig. 38 The structure of the skin.

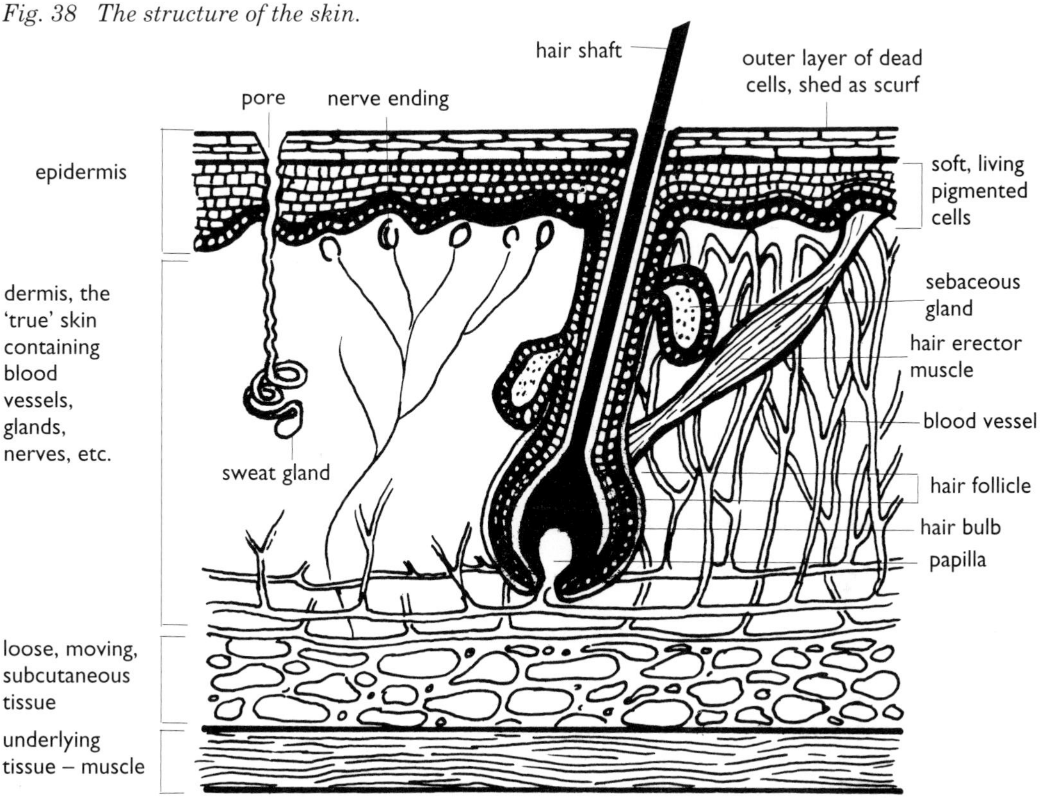

more difficult to recognize. To be safe, any wounds on the back of the lower limbs from knee or hock to the hoof, or in the vicinity of joints (*see* Figs 46 and 47), should be urgently checked by a veterinary surgeon so that appropriate treatment can be instituted if a synovial structure is involved.

Is the Wound in a High-motion Area?
Wounds that are in a high-motion area (i.e. overlying a joint) are particularly difficult to treat. Even when they do not involve the joint itself, their position means that healing may be delayed by any movement of the joint; and if they are sutured, they will be more likely to break down. Prompt veterinary attention should be sought.

Is the Wound on the Lower Limb?
Wounds on the lower limbs (i.e. below the knee or hock) are likely to become contaminated by soil or dung, and should therefore be kept covered whilst awaiting the vet. Prompt veterinary attention should be sought.

How Deep is the Wound?
In order to assess the depth of a wound, it needs to be carefully examined, which in itself may require veterinary attention and sedation. Some knowledge of the anatomy of the skin is necessary (*see* Fig. 38).

In most cases it is necessary to clip the hair away from the wound edges in order to be able to see inside the wound to examine it properly. Squeezing some clean KY

85

jelly into the wound before clipping around it helps to prevent contamination of the wound with hair during clipping. The KY jelly can then easily be flushed out of the wound, carrying hair and other debris with it. A dilute solution of a recommended antiseptic or saline should be used to flush the wound. Sometimes your vet will insert a sterile probe into a deep cavity to assess it better. It may also be necessary to enlarge the wound surgically in order to see deeper damaged tissues and to treat them properly. In some cases, deep sedation or even general anaesthesia is needed to explore the full extent of a deep wound.

Partial-thickness Skin Wounds

Partial-thickness skin wounds may ooze blood, and appear very raw, but if the full thickness of the skin has not been breached, stitching will not be necessary (*see* Abrasions, page 96).

Full-thickness Skin Wounds

A full-thickness skin wound is one where the skin edges can be parted to show underlying tissues. Usually just muscles are visible, but sometimes other structures, such as nerves, blood vessels, and bone, can be seen.

A full-thickness skin wound that involves no deeper structures will usually need stitching. Exceptions to this are those wounds that are extremely small, and can safely be left to heal on their own; those wounds in which an area of skin is missing and therefore cannot be closed (although usually these can at least be partially stitched and thus reduced in size); and those involving a flap of skin, the blood supply of which has been lost, which will therefore in any event die away. Wire wounds to the lower limbs often fall into this category.

Even if you don't think stitching of such a wound is necessary you should seek veterinary attention so that your vet can ensure there is no damage to deeper structures. Anti-tetanus medication may also be required.

Deep Wounds

Wounds involving deeper structures, such as underlying muscles, may require attention under general anaesthesia, particularly if any damage to bone is suspected. Some deep gashes may be best managed as open wounds and not sutured. These can take many months to heal. Others may be possible to suture. In either case prompt veterinary attention is recommended, not only so that your vet can check there is no damage to deeper structures, but so that anti-tetanus medication can be given.

Puncture wounds are deep wounds with only small skin injuries. These should not be stitched, because in many cases infection will have been introduced. In some cases they need to be surgically enlarged or explored, particularly if they are in the vicinity of joints or tendons, to ensure that they do not involve these structures. In most cases they need to be cleaned well, and then poulticed. Prompt veterinary attention is recommended, not only so that your vet can check there is no damage to deeper structures, but so that anti-tetanus medication can be given.

Initial Treatment of Wounds

The initial treatment of wounds should be aimed at either:

• The stabilization of a situation and prevention of further injury whilst awaiting the veterinary surgeon,

or

• The treatment of those wounds that do not require veterinary attention to aid healing.

Tetanus

Tetanus (or 'lockjaw') is a bacterial disease caused by the spores of *Clostridium tetani*, which are ubiquitous in the soil. This means that when even the smallest of wounds becomes contaminated, tetanus is a risk. This applies particularly to lower-limb wounds, which are most likely to become contaminated, and especially those that are puncture wounds where the oxygen-free atmosphere inside the wound encourages the multiplication of tetanus bacteria.

Tetanus toxin inhibits the ability of muscles to relax once they have contracted, and thus results in progressive symptoms of muscle stiffness and then paralysis. It affects the smaller muscles first. Early signs include generalized stiffness and muscle tremors, which tend to be followed by prolapse of the nictating membrane (or 'third eyelid', which moves across from the corner of the eye), and restriction of jaw movements and swallowing (hence the common term 'lockjaw'). Drooling and difficulty in eating or inability to eat are seen, and these signs are followed by constipation, inability to pass urine, the development of a 'saw-horse' stance (*see* Fig. 39), collapse, and finally death from respiratory paralysis.

All horses should be routinely vaccinated against tetanus (*see* Chapter 1). This provides some protective immunity against the disease, but may not provide sufficient protection where deep and obviously contaminated wounds are present. In such cases, an additional tetanus injection should be given within 12 hours. For this reason, all wounds on the legs, and any deep wounds on the body, should be examined and assessed promptly by a vet so that tetanus anti-toxin (ready-made antibodies to tetanus toxin) can be given where necessary. This immediate extra protection is far more effective in preventing the disease than are attempts to treat the disease once it occurs.

Typically tetanus may incubate for one to three weeks after an injury before it starts to cause symptoms, and the progression of these symptoms may be slow over the subsequent one to two weeks. Treatment for tetanus at the stage when it is diagnosed is extremely expensive and rarely successful.

Treatment of tetanus includes debridement of the wound (surgical removal of damaged or contaminated tissues), and antibiotic treatment, as well as the administration of large amounts of tetanus anti-toxin. Tranquillizers and a dark, quiet, calm environment are also helpful, as they reduce muscle stimulation to a minimum and thus slow the progression of the disease. Fluids may need to be given by stomach tube, or intravenously via a drip, to maintain hydration. Despite these measures many horses do not survive. The importance of regular vaccination and prompt attention to wounds cannot be overemphasized.

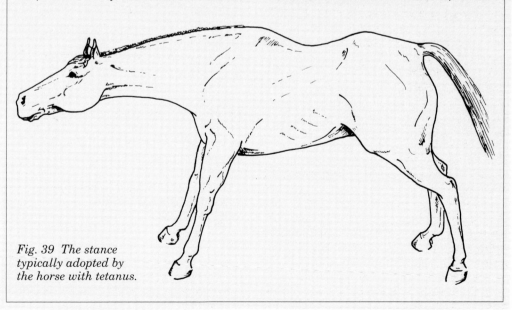

Fig. 39 The stance typically adopted by the horse with tetanus.

It is worth emphasizing that where examination of a wound cannot be carried out without risking human injury, it is worth awaiting the vet who can then give the horse painkillers, sedatives, or tranquillizers as necessary.

Since bleeding from wounds generally appears to be more severe than it is, the tendency to apply a dressing immediately to any wound that is discharging blood is not always the best course of action. Unless blood is spurting or gushing from a wound (in which case a pressure bandage should be applied) it is more important to clean it properly than it is to cover it up.

Cleaning Wounds
Cleaning of wounds should be carried out promptly: the sooner wounds are cleaned the less the chance of their becoming infected. Cleaning is best done with very dilute antiseptic solutions such as a 0.1 per cent povidone iodine (1 measure of Pevidine scrub in 7.5 measures water) or 0.05 per cent chlorhexidine (1 measure of Hibiscrub in 40 measures of water) solutions. If these are not available, saline can be used. This can be made by adding 1 teaspoon of salt to 1 pint (560ml) of clean water. Other antiseptics, or stronger solutions of these ones, can cause further cell damage. Cleaning can be done with clean cotton-wool swabs soaked in antiseptic, or a clean syringe can be used to wash contamination gently out of the wound. Care should be taken not to wash bacteria further into a wound, and for this reason hosing, or high-pressure syringing, is to be avoided. An alternative option is to use a garden sprayer from a garden centre, which provides a suitable amount of pressure.

Veterinary Treatment of Wounds

When your vet arrives, he will probably need to spend a little time assessing your horse, not only to check the extent of all injuries present, but to monitor any signs of pain, shock and blood loss.

and medication to reduce inflammation and swelling as well as pain are often necessary. These may be given in food, or they may need to be injected, depending on the type of drugs that are appropriate for each individual case (*see* Appendix). Intramuscular injections can, in some cases, be given by the horse owner (*see* Appendix), but other medication may need to be given by your vet and may thus necessitate further veterinary visits or hospitalization.

Medication
Whether or not your vet needs to suture any wounds, antibiotics and anti-tetanus medication are likely to be given. In addition, painkillers and sedatives may be given by injection into the horse's veins or muscles. The use of sedatives or tranquillizers will make a horse drowsy and reduce his anxiety, thus making examination and treatment easier. Side-effects such as wobbliness and sweating may be seen.

After the initial veterinary treatment has been carried out, ongoing antibiotics

Suturing
When making the decision whether or not to suture a wound, your vet will have in mind the aim of suturing, which is whether or not stitching the wound will ultimately be helpful.

Wounds that require suturing need to be seen promptly because within a few hours of the wound's occurring its edges start to contract and lose their ability to knit together. If the wound is not fresh (less than 24 hours old) it may be necessary to enlarge it by cutting back the edges to fresh tissue, otherwise it may not heal. Similarly, if the edges of the wound are particularly frayed or otherwise damaged, their blood supply may be lost, and the skin edges may need to be cut back to healthy tissue before the wound is sutured. Any contamination of a wound starts to cause infection within four to six hours. This can prevent healing of the wound as infection produces pus beneath the surface and the suture line. Production of other fluids (such as blood or serum) from beneath the suture-line can also cause distraction of the wound edges if not allowed to drain. In addition, wounds that lie in high-motion areas, such as over joints, may be subjected to distracting forces caused by movements of the skin as the leg moves, which may prevent healing at the suture-line.

This means that wounds that are not fresh, or that are particularly deep or contaminated, or that overlie high-motion areas, are likely to break down if they are sutured. It may be, however, that the resulting area of skin deficit will be smaller than that of the original wound, and so will heal faster, so it may still be advisable to stitch such a wound.

From an aesthetic point of view, many horse owners are extremely keen that suturing is carried out because a wound that heals successfully after stitching scars less than one that is managed without suturing. However, it is important for horse owners' expectations of the outcome of wound-suturing to be realistic. Even with the neatest stitches and the best care, many wounds cannot be prevented from breaking down and re-opening, and a wound that has been sutured and then breaks down may scar more than one that was initially managed as an open wound. In many ways it is better to prepare yourself for the worst and to expect that a wound will break down, need months of nursing care, and will scar, than to expect it to heal within a few weeks.

Shallow Wounds
As a general rule, wounds that are small (less than 1in/2–3cm) and involve the skin only in low-motion areas may equally well be either left to heal alone or sutured after cleaning, although suturing such wounds is likely to speed up the healing time slightly.

Small wounds involving only the skin may be able to be sutured using only local anaesthetic, although in most cases sedation is necesssary to allow a horse to be comfortable, calm and still enough for suturing to be carried out. In some horses a nose twitch is also used to aid comfort and tranquillity.

Larger wounds that involve the skin only, and with skin available to close across the gap, may be sutured, but they may break down if swelling, infection, or excessive movement in the area occur.

Deep Wounds
Larger and deeper wounds should be sutured only if they can be thoroughly cleaned and if the deeper tissues as well as the skin can be accessed and stitched. If several layers of muscle are damaged, they will need to be sewn together to re-create their structure before the skin is closed. This may require surgical enlargement of the skin wound so that sufficient access to these deeper structures is possible.

With these larger wounds in particular, gaps can be left in the skin suture-line for drainage of any fluid, or, better still, a drain can be placed within the wound for the first few days of healing. The drain needs to be sutured into the deepest part of the wound to allow any fluid that builds up to escape without putting pressure on the stitch-line. As well as allowing drainage out of a wound, however, a drain can allow infection to be led into a wound, and so must be used with care, kept clean, and removed as soon as possible. Where discharge from a wound or a drain occurs, petroleum jelly should be applied to the skin beneath to prevent scalding.

Large wounds with skin deficits should be managed as open wounds, or may be partially sutured to reduce the size of the skin deficit. Puncture wounds should never be sutured, but rather should be cleaned thoroughly before poulticing and should be allowed to heal by secondary intention (*see* box, below).

Open Wounds
An open wound heals by secondary intention, and so complete healing can take a long time, depending on the size of the wound. With no complications, for example, a 1½in (4cm) diameter skin deficit in a low-motion area may easily take four to six weeks to heal, and similar wounds in a high-motion area may take several months. In addition, the healed skin is likely to remain as a scar, and may never grow hair, or, if it does, may well grow white hair and thus remain unsightly.

Primary and secondary intention healing

Primary intention healing refers to the knitting together of adjacent tissues when they are brought into close proximity (as is the case when a wound is sutured and does not break down). It can result in healing in as short a time as one to two weeks. Secondary intention healing is a more time-consuming process that involves the filling of the base of a wound with healing 'granulation' tissue, and the subsequent growth of a layer of skin across the wound (epidermalization). Once a base of granulation tissue fills the wound, epidermalization begins, and the skin edges can grow towards one another by as much as 1⁄16in (1–2mm) a day if the conditions are right.

The management of open wounds relies on regular daily cleaning, bandaging, and the use of certain medication. Bandages and dressings are used to keep a wound clean until a full bed of granulation tissue fills the base of the wound and protects underlying tissues, and can also be used to reduce movement in the area which can otherwise slow healing. The formation of granulation tissue can be encouraged by packing the wound with gels (such as Intrasite). Granulation tissue has a rough, pink, appearance and has little sensation (*see* Fig. 40).

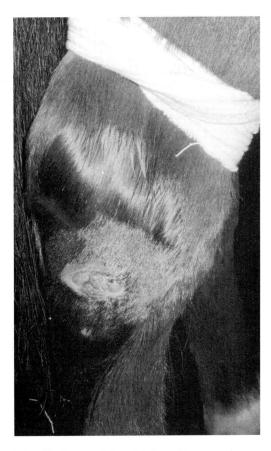

Fig. 40 A wound in a high-motion area (near the hock) with exuberant granulation tissue (proud flesh).

Epidermalization of an open wound is slowed by movement of the tissue in the area of the wound, and by the presence of infection, swelling and inflammation. For this reason it is important to:

1. Control infection with antibiotics.
2. Control inflammation and swelling with anti-inflammatory medication where necessary.
3. Immobilize the area.

Infection and movement of the tissues involved in a wound can also contribute to the development of exuberant amounts of granulation tissue (see Fig. 40). If the granulation tissue develops to such an extent that it bulges beyond the surface of the wound, it is described as proud flesh. This then slows, or can prevent, the healing of the wound. It may need to be cut back surgically, or burnt back using caustic powder, to allow skin healing to occur. It is important to use caustic powder with care. Only small quantities are required; if too much is used a deep burn may result. Caustic powder must be applied only to the granulation tissue because if it is allowed to contact the healing edge of the wound it can damage the skin edge and prevent it from growing across.

Bandaging

Bandaging of wounds (both open and sutured) can fulfil a variety of aims (see Chapter 4). Dressings can be used to help protect a wound from further contamination and trauma, as well as to help reduce swelling, and to aid pain relief by helping to immobilize the area. Dressings can prevent a horse from attacking a wound when it is itchy or painful, particularly during the healing phase, although a muzzle may be needed to prevent the horse removing it with his teeth. Covering a wound helps to reduce fluid loss, as well as aiding healing

by causing an increase in temperature and acidity of the tissue within the wound. It is important not to apply a bandage too tightly, however, or the blood supply to the area may be reduced, which can slow healing or cause further damage.

The appropriate dressing of other wounds depends largely on their type. Puncture wounds should be poulticed for the first few days, or until the pus is no longer seen on the poultice. Animalintex soaked in warm water and bandaged over the wound works very well. Such a dressing should be changed twice daily.

Wounds on high-motion areas, such as joints, are often best covered with a thick, firm dressing that reduces or prevents the horse's ability to bend the affected area, thus reducing the application of distracting forces across the wound.

Wounds on the lower limbs should be covered with a light dressing to keep them clean, and all wounds are best covered with a light dressing to protect them from dirt and flies. Such bandages are generally best changed twice daily, but if no infection is present they may be able to be left for up to three or four days between changes. If bandages are to be left on for several days they must be applied carefully to avoid slipping. Padding must be used to prevent pressure, and tight dressings must be applied all the way down to the hoof to prevent swelling of the foot and pastern caused by fluid build-up.

Slow Healing and Wound Breakdown

There are various factors that will adversely affect the speed of healing, or cause a wound to break down. These include:

Movement
Restrict the horse and dress the wound to prevent mobilization.

Infection
Clean all wounds as soon as possible, and keep them clean. Use antibiotics promptly where necessary.

Tissue damage
Check the wound regularly for signs of tissues desiccation within the wound, and use only approved antiseptics at approved dilutions to avoid causing tissue damage.

Discharge
Where discharge (whether serum, blood or pus) is being produced from a wound then either appropriate measures should be taken to halt its formation, or its drainage should be encouraged.

Swelling
Swelling and inflammation can cause the edges of a wound to pull apart. Swelling should be kept under control by bandaging, cold hosing, and the prompt use of anti-inflammatory drugs as appropriate.

Fly strike

During the summer months, any open wound that is oozing fluid acts as a magnet to flies. Blowflies in particular (*see* page 98) are attracted to such wounds, and lay their eggs in them; these then hatch into maggots within 12 to 24 hours. The contamination of open wounds with fly eggs and maggots is referred to as fly strike, and can cause exacerbation of a wound, as well as further contamination, predisposing them to the development of proud flesh, and causing considerable distress to the horse. Fly strike is best avoided by covering such wounds (where possible) with dressings, using fly repellents, and using wound powders which contain chemicals that prevent the development of fly eggs.

Proud flesh
The development of exuberant granulation tissue (or proud flesh) is usually related to delayed wound-healing caused by infection, mobilization, etc. A vicious circle can develop. Where present, proud flesh should be dealt with promptly by surgical debridement or the application of caustic substances to burn it back.

Healing of wounds is aided by resting the horse, preferably restricting him to a box. Wounds in high-motion areas may also be encouraged to heal if the horse is prevented from lying down, and kept as still as possible during the initial healing phase. Cross-tying the horse in a stable to prevent him from being able to move around, cruel though this sounds, can vastly reduce the healing time of such wounds.

Special Cases

Specific types of wound that commonly occur often behave in predictable ways, and so are worth discussing further.

Hoof-wall Wounds
Hoof-wall wounds are a special case, since healing cannot occur by the knitting together of tissues.
The hoof is continually produced from the coronary band. An injury causing a deficit in the hoof wall (commonly either an overreach or a wire wound) can be difficult to treat. If the coronary band is damaged, a permanent hoof-wall deficit can result, and the hoof may grow down with a full-length crack from the site of the coronary band injury. If the coronary band is not affected, the most important thing is to provide protection of the underlying tissues, and stability to the hoof and to the edges of the deficit. If stability is not provided, the edges of hoof that are intact will

93

continue to move relative to one another, and a permanent crack may result.

In most cases the best results are gained by applying a supportive shoe such as an egg-bar or straight-bar shoe, and by bridging the hoof-wall deficit to prevent movement. In the case of narrow cracks, this may be achieved with wire staples or sutures. Where wider deficits are present, packing with fibreglass may also be necessary, and a fibreglass hoof cast may be applied round the entire hoof to aid stability and give the best chance of immobilization. If immobilization is achieved, the hoof-wall deficit will then grow down towards the weight-bearing surface of the hoof, and eventually grow out.

Overreach Wounds

Overreach wounds in the heel or pastern area (caused when a hind hoof strikes the fore) often result from movement at speed in muddy conditions, and are usually dirty and deep, with extensive tissue damage. Veterinary treatment should be sought urgently as there is a risk of deep digital flexor tendon involvement in the pastern area. Those injuries in the area of the heels generally avoid deeper structures.

Copious bleeding from these wounds may suggest involvement of the palmar digital arteries, and pressure dressings encasing the entire foot may be needed for up to ten days to stop the bleeding and allow healing. Extensive tissue damage, lack of spare skin in this area, likely contamination, and the difficulty or impossibility of achieving immobilization of the area mean that it is rarely appropriate to suture these wounds. Instead, they are generally managed as open wounds, although suturing can occasionally be carried out. In either case the area should be cleaned regularly, kept covered with bandages and, as far as possible, immobilized. Box-rest is therefore advisable for at least a week to allow the initial healing phase

to be completed rapidly. Anti-tetanus medication is advisable, and antibiotics are likely to be needed.

It is important to bear in mind that nerve damage, either temporary or permanent, can accompany arterial damage since the vein and artery lie side by side. The horse may thus be left with poor foot sensation.

Brushing Injuries

Brushing injuries, or other wounds in the area of the back of the lower limb, can easily involve the underlying tendons or tendon sheaths. Where severe tendon injury is present the fetlock may lose its support and take on a 'dropped' appearance. Any wounds in this area should be seen urgently by a vet so that tendon-sheath injury can be recognized promptly and dealt with appropriately.

Extensive lavage of the wound is necessary, and this may require general anaesthesia. Initial cleaning can be carried out in the yard, but if transportation to an equine hospital is needed this should be carried out without delay. Splinting or dressing of the limb for the journey may well be necessary to prevent further damage.

If the injury does not involve the tendons or tendon sheaths, suturing may be necessary to close skin deficits. Those injuries in which degloving of the area occurs (i.e. a large skin deficit results) can be extremely serious, since loss of large amounts of skin can result in damage to the underlying tissues via fluid loss. Drying out (desiccation) of underlying bone, for instance, can result in damage to the surface of the bone. Consequent loss of blood supply to the bone surface can then cause areas of bone to die off. Although some breakdown of the wound is to be expected in such cases, attempts to suture it are to be encouraged. The covering of exposed areas with skin aids their granulation, as long as gross contamination has been removed. In addition, uncovered areas should be treated with a moist gel to prevent desiccation of the area, and antibiotics should be given. These wounds are usually in high-motion areas, so immobilization of the area is likely to be necessary to aid healing. Box-rest and support dressings may well be needed if wound breakdown and the development of proud flesh are to be avoided. Anti-tetanus medication, antibiotics and anti-inflammatories are all likely to be needed.

Wounds in the Vicinity of Joints

Wounds in the vicinity of joints need similarly to be assessed promptly by a vet. In many cases these take the form of horizontal lacerations or flap wounds. In either case the ability to heal may be affected by reduction of blood supply to the lower-wound edge since much of the blood supply runs vertically. In addition, flap wounds may result in complete loss of blood supply to the triangular flap, which can result in the death of this area and wound breakdown if suturing is attempted. It is usually worth suturing these wounds, though, as even if the wound does partially break down it usually leaves a smaller deficit. Again support dressings are needed if wound breakdown and proud flesh are to be avoided. If the wound becomes infected, though, the infection can build up under the pressure bandage and cause intense pain. Any signs of increasing lameness or swelling above or below the bandage may indicate that infection is present, so bandage removal is advisable to allow the wound to be checked.

Puncture Wounds

Puncture wounds on any part of the body should never be sutured or covered with a pressure bandage. Instead, they should be examined promptly to ensure that their extent does not involve deeper structures, and then should be cleaned as well as possible and poulticed to aid removal of infection rather than locking it in.

Animalintex soaked in warm water and applied directly to the wound is usually the most appropriate poulticing material. This can be bandaged in place over a wound, and changed twice daily until no more discharge is seen. Where puncture wounds cannot be effectively poulticed because of their position, they should be washed out twice daily and otherwise allowed to drain. Application of petroleum jelly to the skin below prevents scalding from discharge. Most puncture wounds necessitate treatment with anti-tetanus medication, and most also need antibiotic treatment.

Puncture wounds of the sole of the foot are likely to result in the development of a sub-solar abcess, unless the foot is pared to allow drainage. All horses with solar punctures should be examined to ensure that there is no involvement of the pedal bone or navicular bone, since infection of these areas can be untreatable, and is potentially fatal.

Head and neck wounds
These should always be investigated rapidly (*see* Chapter 6), and the likelihood of the involvement of deeper structures should be assessed.

Chest and abdominal wounds
These are rarely serious, but if they are deep, and if discharges such as frothy fluid from chest wounds, or clear fluid from abdominal wounds (*see* Chapter 10), are seen, the likelihood of penetration of the chest and abdominal cavities respectively must be considered.

Vulval wounds
These are often seen post foaling, and may need to be sutured within 12 hours of birth. Deeper wounds are rare.

Gunshot Wounds

Gunshot wounds are, in most respects, comparable to puncture wounds and should be treated as such. In most cases deep wounds are present under the skin, infection has been introduced, and fragments of shot remaining within the body are a potentially ongoing source of infection. Such fragments may be removed, but in many cases this is impossible. The potential for injury of deeper structures, including bones, joints, and soft tissues, should also be taken seriously. Gunshot wounds should always be examined by a vet as antibiotics are likely to be necessary.

ABRASIONS

Abrasions are like wounds but do not usually involve full-thickness skin damage. Instead they are like grazes. Loss of the superficial layers of skin is seen, and exudation of fluid and blood from the surface may occur. These injuries are often caused by blunt trauma, and often involve much swelling and bruising of the underlying tissue. Like wounds, they should be cleaned with dilute antiseptics as described above. Antibiotic and anti-tetanus medications are rarely necessary if a full-thickness skin injury is not present, but anti-inflammatory medication may be needed to control swelling and inflammation. Rest and immobilization of the area will aid healing, and the use of topical lotions and gels (such as Intrasite) to prevent fluid loss and drying of the area can help to speed healing.

Most saddle sores and girth galls fall into this category, and need to be treated in this way. In addition, the area may be hardened up once healing has taken place by the application of saline or surgical spirit. Complete healing should be allowed before using tack that applies any pressure to the affected area.

BURNS

In many ways burns are like any other kind of skin wound. Superficial burns lead to reddening and tenderness of the skin, and swelling may also be seen. Partial-thickness burns are characterized by raw, blistered skin, and full-thickness burns have a waxy, charred appearance.

Loss of the superficial layers of skin result in the presence of an open wound. However, charring of the tissues results in overwhelming inflammation of affected areas and loss of plasma (protein-containing fluid that leaks from the surrounding blood vessels) from the open areas. It is this loss of plasma that is ultimately most dangerous for horses, for it can lead to the development of circulatory shock. In cases where more than 30 per cent of the body is affected by full-thickness burns, it is unusual for the horse to survive for more than 24 to 48 hours after the injuries were sustained. This is because the damage caused to the circulatory system and to the kidneys by plasma loss will be extensive in such cases.

With any burns the priority is to reduce plasma loss and to promote cooling of the area. The wounds should therefore be covered as soon as possible with cool, wet dressings to encourage granulation. The specially designed dressings containing a gel-like substance are best suited to this function, but if you do not have any of these you will need to soak pieces of clean cloth or towelling. In addition, medical treatment with high doses of anti-inflammatories to reduce swelling, fluid exudation and pain, and intravenous fluid therapy to replace fluid lost into the burned tissue, is necessary to maintain the circulation.

It is also important to remember that affected horses are likely also to be suffering from smoke inhalation, and possibly internal burns through inhalation of hot smoke (see Chapter 9). Such horses may also need medication to aid breathing.

Photosensitivity and Sunburn

Although it occurs only rarely in horses in the UK, sunburn can be very difficult to treat. In the absence of underlying disease, it tends to be seen on the hairless de-pigmented areas of skin such as the muzzle and lower limbs. It is a normal response to excessive exposure to sunlight, particularly that in the UV-B range, and its occurrence depends on a combination of the strength of the sunlight, the degree of skin protection by hair and by skin pigments such as melanin, and the presence or absence of presensitizing substances within the skin. Sunburn causes inflammation within the skin, resulting in reddening, swelling, the leakage of inflammatory fluid, and thus the formation of blisters. Scabbing follows, and secondary infection can occur. The treatment of such blisters should include withdrawal from the sun while healing occurs, as well as the use of medication.

Whenever sunburn is seen, photosensitization should be considered a possible cause. In the British climate, primary sunburn is rare, and in most cases it is likely that a predisposing factor is involved. Photosensitization (sensitization to light) of the skin renders it much more liable to burning on exposure to the sun. In particular, photosensitization causes an excessive reaction to light in the UV-A range. This means that a small amount of sunlight can result in a very severe inflammatory reaction that progresses rapidly from the formation of crusty vesicles to the development of open, and sometimes bleeding, sores. Healing of these can result in the formation of scar tissue.

Photosensitivity may be primary or secondary in origin, depending on whether it is caused directly by the production of photo-active chemicals (ones that are stimulated to undergo a chemical reaction by light) in the body, or by another disease process.

Primary photosensitization follows the digestion of certain plants or the metabolism of particular drugs that release photo-active chemicals. Plants with these properties include St John's Wort (*Hypericum* species) and Buckwheat (*Fagopyrum* species), and (in large quantities) the Brassicas (the cabbage family of plants), lupins, alfalfa, clovers (*Trifolium* species) and vetch, as well as Bog Asphodel, Charlock and Ragwort (*Senecio jacobea*).

Secondary photosensitivity usually results from liver disease, which causes the amounts of normal products of plant digestion in the blood to rise to levels that can cause photosensitivity. (This is because the liver is no longer able to detoxify and remove these compounds.) Photosensitivity associated with internal toxins can result in extensive lesions across the whole body, particularly in grey horses and those with areas of white skin. Normal sunburn, however, is usually limited to unpigmented areas on the back and the face. In some cases skin contact with certain plants can cause localized areas of sensitivity to light; this is seen particularly on the lower limbs and face.

Treatment of both the underlying or predisposing cause, and the resulting disease, must be undertaken. Skin lesions will usually require anti-inflammatory and antibiotic treatment. Affected horses should be stabled away from sunlight during daytime, and any access to plants that contain photo-active pigments should be prevented. Where photosensitivity occurs secondarily to liver disease, this should be treated with vitamin and mineral supplementation, a low-protein diet, and rest; unfortunately, anti-inflammatory treatment should be avoided as it may further stress the liver. High-factor sunblock can be used on horses to prevent sunburn where the risk of it is localized to small areas such as the muzzle.

SKIN DISEASES

Allergic Skin Disease

Although relatively uncommon in the horse, skin disease caused by allergies can occur either through skin contact with substances to which the horse is allergic (shavings, for example), or through ingestion of a substance to which he is sensitive. Horses can develop allergies to any of a range of foodstuffs from sugar-beet pulp to high-protein concentrates.

Symptoms include the development of urticarial lesions ('hives'), which look like fine blisters under the skin. Itching of these areas can result in their opening to form oozing sores.

In either case anti-inflammatory medication is needed to treat the weals. The substance causing allergic skin disease should be identified by trial and error or intradermal skin testing. In the case of food allergies, alfalfa hay is widely accepted to be relatively hypo-allergenic and can therefore be used in an exclusion diet. When the symptoms have subsided, other foods can be added in one at a time until the culprit is identified.

Parasitic Disease of the Skin

Skin injuries can relate to some parasitic diseases. External parasites can cause skin disease directly, and/or their presence can cause itching, inducing the horse to scratch himself and so damage the skin.

Blowflies

Blowflies (see Fly Strike, page 93) can cause problems in horses. They lay their eggs in fresh wounds, whether of surgical or accidental origin, and the resulting larvae (maggots) hatch within a few hours to devour the wounded tissue. If not treated, infected wounds can turn into more severe,

deeper and non-healing wounds that usually become secondarily infected with bacteria. Control requires the use of fly repellents and drugs that prevent maggots from hatching, and treatment involves regular cleaning and flushing of open wounds to remove dead tissue as well as eggs and maggots.

Stable-flies, Black-flies, Horn-flies, Horse-flies and Mosquitoes

All these flies will attack horses in large numbers, causing painful bleeding weals where the mouthparts of the fly tear the horse's skin to feed on blood. The bites can become crusty sores that take a long time to heal, particularly in those horses that have a sensitivity to the saliva of the fly. The flies can also infect the horse with *Habronema*, a larva that lives in the skin and causes 'summer sores'. These are lesions, which can be seen around the eyes and the genitals in particular. They cause intense itching, and their open, weeping appearance attracts more flies. Stable-flies feed during the daytime and are a particular problem to those horses stabled during the day. They are attracted by dirty bedding, so their control is aided by good stable hygiene, as well as the use of fly repellents and insecticides.

Botflies

These cause mild irritation as they lay their eggs on the hair of the legs and face. The bots (eggs) are taken into the mouth as the horse grooms himself. They then hatch, and the larvae migrate through the tissues of the mouth (sometimes causing lesions on the tongue or in the salivary glands). They pass to the stomach where they attach themselves to the wall but rarely cause disease, and larvae are passed in the faeces. Grooming of the eggs from the horse's hairs can prevent the horse from infecting himself with bots, or the parasite can be treated within the horse using a wormer that is effective against bots (*see* Chapter 1).

Midges

Midges can cause symptoms ranging from mild irritation and head-shaking to sweet itch in susceptible individuals (those allergic to the *Culicoides* midge saliva). As these midges are seen mostly during the hotter months of the year, sweet itch tends to be seen only in the summer months, although severely affected animals may suffer all year round. In the worst case it can even constitute unsoundness as it can prevent animals from being ridden. It is characterized by intense itching (pruritis) and subsequent hair loss (alopecia), which is seen in particular in the skin of the ears, mane and tail-base areas, and often also on the top of the back. Rubbing of these areas to relieve irritation results in loss and matting of hair, tissue damage, and further inflammation. Small bumps may be seen in the skin in the early stages, but these are rapidly converted into plaques of inflamed and weeping tissue that becomes thickened and scabby. Ponies that suffer from the disease year after year will often be seen to have particularly thickened skin in these areas, even in winter, and the hair may not grow properly in these places.

Treatment includes the use of anti-inflammatory and antibiotic medications to reduce the inflammatory response, and to aid healing of the affected areas, as well as avoidance of the midges both by management (stabling during the early mornings and late evenings when the midges are about), and use of fly repellents and insecticides.

Lice

There are two main types of louse: biting and sucking. Both types are up to about ⅛in (3mm) in length and so can be seen with the naked eye. Both cause intense skin irritation, but whilst sucking lice live on serous fluid exuded by damaged skin, biting lice live on blood, and severe infestations with these can result in anaemia and weight loss.

Lice are seen most commonly in the winter months, and their predilection areas are among the coarse hairs of the mane and tail, although in severe infestations they can be found all over the body. The intense irritation and itching induced by the parasites causes the horse to rub the affected areas, often until the skin becomes raw. Careful examination of affected horses reveals the presence of lice and nits, which are most easily seen with a torch and a magnifying glass. Transmission is usually made by direct contact, although particularly in the egg form (as nits) they can be spread on grooming equipment or fences and stables. The nits can also remain dormant in the environment for long periods of time. Treatment involves the use of permethrin-based washes or powders, which kill the adult lice but must be repeated 10 to 14 days later to kill the matured nits. It is a good idea to treat fencing and stables at the same time.

Mange

Mange is caused by any one of several different species of mite. Mange mites are tiny insects that cannot be seen on the skin with the naked eye but can be seen under a microscope on samples of skin scrapings. The mites live in the skin and are usually spread only by direct contact. They are rare in horses in the UK, but can cause severe irritation with consequent loss of condition. Some of the several different species of mange mite are easier to treat than others. Their identification can be carried out using microscopy. The commonest type of horse mange in the UK is chorioptic mange, which affects the legs in particular. It causes intense itching, and when the affected horse scratches and rubs the areas scaly and crusty lesions develop, mostly on the lower hind legs. These can be treated relatively easily with pyrethroid sprays and washes.

Ringworm

Ringworm is a fungal skin infection that can also cause severe itching and thus skin injury through self-excoriation. It is usually spread by direct contact, but it can be carried on grooming equipment or fencing and stables. Since the incubation period can be anywhere between one and four weeks, it is often the case that a whole yard of horses becomes affected after the introduction of one who is carrying the disease. In addition, it can be transmitted to humans.

Lesions are characteristically small, round, itchy spots, which widen and become crusty before hair is lost in the area. They can occur anywhere on the body. Diagnosis can often be carried out merely by inspecting the lesions, but in some cases scrapings of skin need to be taken for microscopy and culture. Although cases are usually self-limiting in that horses tend to develop immunity and spontaneously recover, treatment is usually instituted to achieve a quicker result. This can consist of either washes or in-feed medication.

Mud Fever and Rain-Scald

Both these diseases are caused by infection of the skin with a bacteria called *Dermatophilus congolensis*. The term rain-scald is used when lesions are on the body, and the name mud fever when lesions affect the heels and feet. The bacteria is present on the skin of normal and healthy horses, and to cause skin infection and disease it needs the presence of small wounds or areas of skin trauma. Such conditions might arise from rubbing caused by boots or ill-fitting bandages or tack, or from predisposing damage to the skin caused by skin parasites, poor clipping technique, or minor wounds. Penetration of the skin by the organism is aided by softening of the skin in wet conditions, hence the common name of the condition. Any horse can be affected, but the disease is generally seen in horses of poor condition, particularly those animals with long shaggy coats and feathers, as these trap moisture.

The lesions are areas of crusting and scabbing, beneath which lie open sores. Typically, the scabs lift with hairs attached. Antibiotic medication may be necessary, but mild cases can respond to topical antiseptic or antibacterial washes.

Self-Excoriation

Some skin conditions produce itchiness that then causes horses to damage themselves by scratching. This is occasionally seen in horses with neurological disease, as the condition causes abnormal skin sensation that then drives the horse to scratch at an area of skin that would be otherwise healthy.

Boredom can also cause horses to damage themselves. Stallions in particular can develop the habit of chewing an area of the body, often the flank or stifle, if they are insufficiently stimulated and exercised.

Any type of skin disease that causes self-damage requires the use of medication to reduce inflammation and pain associated with the lesions, as well as treatment of the root cause of the self-damage. If not, a vicious circle is set up in which the damage causes inflammation, which causes further irritation, which stimulates more self-damage.

9 Neck and Chest Injuries

Injuries of the neck, chest and the thoracic organs are uncommon in the horse (the limbs and head are far more vulnerable), but they can occur, particularly when horses run into a fence or a jump. The potential for damage to deeper structures in this area (*see* Fig. 41) means that these injuries should be carefully assessed. Wounds of varying depths, fractures, and heart or lung problems can occur. In addition, internal injuries can follow the ingestion or inhalation of foreign objects.

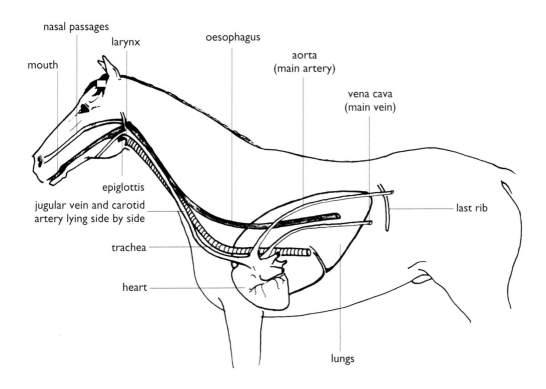

Fig. 41 The soft-tissue structures of the neck and chest.

CHOKE

One of the commonest forms of throat injury is caused by the choke – obstruction of the oesophagus, usually with food particles.

In most cases choke is caused by the feeding of unsoaked or poorly soaked sugar-beet pulp, but it can also occur if any type of food is eaten too fast, particularly if it is dry. The shape of the oesophagus predisposes it to blockage. There are three main predilection sites. The first is at the thoracic inlet, or entrance to the chest cavity at the base of the neck; the second is the point at which the oesophagus tips up to pass over the heart; and the third is at the entrance to the stomach.

The symptoms manifested by horses affected with choke include pain and distress, and a tendency to breathe heavily and to make repeated attempts to swallow, typically with pronounced stretching of the neck. Some particularly greedy horses do continue to attempt to eat, which can exacerbate the problem by progressively blocking up the oesophagus towards the neck. Difficulty in swallowing can result in food material passing down the nose.

Treatment

Treatment is not always necessary, but, since the potential for serious complications is considerable, the vet should always be called immediately. Reassurance (and withdrawal of further food) is all that can be provided until the vet arrives (by which time the choke may have cleared spontaneously). Sedation and the insertion of a stomach tube (which often causes a mild nose bleed) usually clears the blockage. Long-standing blockages can cause damage to the lining of the oesophagus (see page 103), as can the act of unblocking the oesophagus with a stomach tube. Another secondary problem may be pneumo-nia caused by inhalation of food particles and saliva, so antibiotics may be needed.

WOUNDS

Wounds that involve only the skin are rarely serious, although they may need suturing if they are more than 1 inch (2–3cm) long, particularly if they are overlying any important areas such as the jugular vein. More detailed information on how to deal with skin injuries is given in Chapter 8.

Wounds that involve deeper tissue are more serious. They may affect the muscles beneath the skin, the oesophagus, the jugular vein or the trachea if they are located on the underside of the neck, or they may even go deep enough to puncture the lining of the chest cavity and potentially damage the lungs or heart. It is the possible involvement of these deeper structures that makes these wounds such a cause for concern. If there is any question at all as to whether a wound involves only the skin, or also affects deeper structures, it should be investigated further by a vet as soon as possible.

Neck Wounds

Wounds involving the trachea (or wind pipe – which runs down the underside of the neck and can be felt as a firm tube in this position), the oesophagus (gullet), jugular veins, carotid arteries or guttural pouches (which lie just behind the angle of the jaw) are potentially fatal and should be considered to be emergencies.

The Trachea
Tracheal wounds can usually be recognized by escaping air causing bubbling and frothing of blood at the wound; air may also escape into the surrounding skin,

causing swelling and crackling of the tissues in the area. Depending on the extent of the injury, suturing of the trachea may or may not be necessary and possible.

The Oesophagus

The oesophagus runs down the left-hand side of the neck in most horses. It can normally be seen only when a horse swallows a large bolus of food, and this causes a swelling to pass down the left-hand side of the neck. Injuries involving the oesophagus are very serious because of the very poor healing ability of the wall of the structure. Even the smallest puncture can lead to leakage of the oesophageal wall. For this reason, any injuries in the vicinity of the oesophagus – even without obvious symptoms of damage – should be assessed by a vet to ensure that penetration of the oesophagus is not present. Oesophageal injuries can follow severe choke, the swallowing of sharp objects, or external wounds in the area. These cases hold a poor prognosis for recovery.

Symptoms of oesophageal injuries include the leakage of swallowed saliva through the oesophageal wall deficit, which can cause neck swelling, and the appearance of saliva at the skin if an external wound is present. If the horse continues to eat, food material may also be lost through the skin. This is an extremely bad sign.

The Jugular Veins and Carotid Arteries

Injuries involving the jugular veins are obviously serious, and can be life-threatening. Jugular vein injury is indicated by a wound on the underside of the neck, from which copious quantities of blood gush. The jugular is a large vein, which means that a horse can easily bleed to death. Any wound from which blood issues in this manner should receive urgent veterinary attention.

In the meantime, pressure can be applied to the area to try to reduce blood loss.

The carotid arteries lie deeper within the neck than the jugular veins, and run up through the guttural pouches to reach the head. Their damage causes uncontrollable blood loss. The vet should be called immediately and, again, pressure applied.

NECK INJURIES

It is important to bear in mind that injuries to the neck can occur without visible external damage. Swelling or bruising can cause damage to, or occlusion of, the trachea, the oesophagus, and the guttural pouches, even if the skin is not lacerated and a visible wound is not present. Any injuries in the neck area, and in particular those involving the underside of the neck, should therefore be investigated if excessive swelling is present, or the horse is having difficulty breathing.

Swallowed or inhaled foreign bodies can pass in through the nose or mouth and cause damage in the throat. Objects such as pieces of twig can become lodged in the throat or the trachea, and can respectively cause difficulty swallowing or difficulty breathing, as well as signs of pain and distress.

Damage to the hyoid apparatus (which forms the bony part of the larynx) can also cause difficulty swallowing, and this can follow tongue-tying to prevent horses from displacing their soft palate when racing.

Injuries of the musculoskeletal structures of the neck, including the spine, are discussed in Chapter 6.

CHEST INJURIES

In the chest area there are few superficial structures that can be damaged easily because the chest organs are encased within the thoracic spine and the ribcage,

103

which together afford them some protection from injuries.

The Brisket

The thoracic inlet is the name given to the area where the structures of the neck enter the chest cavity. This is a point that is vulnerable because there is a gap in the bony cage which surrounds the chest organs. Injuries in this area should be treated carefully because of the proximity of the heart and lungs, as well as the main arteries and veins to the head, the oesophagus and the trachea. These injuries are seen occasionally when horses run on to a stake or other protruding object. Such injuries may cause damage to the skin and underlying muscle alone, but if excessive bleeding or signs of a tracheal or oesophageal injury are seen (see page 103), injury to deeper structures may have occurred. In such cases a vet should be called, and in the meantime first aid should be carried out (see Chapter 4).

The Walls of the Chest

Injuries involving the walls of the chest may only involve the skin and underlying muscle. Many low-velocity injuries will be prevented from penetrating deeper by the ribs, although objects can penetrate between the ribs to enter the chest cavity, or may even cause rib fracture in the process. Fractures of the ribs generally do not require surgical intervention. They may cause the development of lumps in the area when they have healed, which may have implications concerning the ease of fitting a saddle to the horse, but, other than causing pain and distress, they rarely cause major complications and generally heal with rest alone. The exception to this occurs when fragments of fractured ribs penetrate deeper into the chest cavity, and can themselves cause further injury. Cases in which penetration of the heart or lungs occurs in this way are not unknown.

Penetration of the Chest Cavity

Even though few clinical signs (other than the presence of a wound over the chest area) may be seen in the immediate aftermath of an injury, penetration of the chest cavity (whether with a rib fragment or another object or foreign body) can be serious. It can result in inflammation and may allow infection of the pleural cavity which surrounds the lungs (causing pleuritis or pleurisy).

If the lungs themselves are penetrated, air is allowed to leak into the pleural space and thence out through the wound. This results in a similar appearance to that of tracheal wounds, because the released air manifests itself by causing frothing of fluid at the wound and leaking into the surrounding tissues, which then take on a crackly texture. In addition, leakage of air from the lungs can lead to partial or complete collapse of the lung involved, and consequent difficulty breathing. This can be an emergency.

Penetration of the heart, or its major blood vessels, causes acute and severe bleeding, and is likely to be fatal. Bleeding may be seen from the wound itself, and blood may also be seen pouring from the nose, and even the mouth.

The Lungs

Bleeding from the nose can also be seen if minor blood vessels in the lungs are damaged. This can occur following injuries to the chest, but can also occur following injuries in which there are no serious sign of chest trauma. An injury caused by running into a blunt object at high velocity, such as a jump, can cause minor signs of bleeding from the nose even without major chest trauma.

Exercise-Induced Pulmonary Haemorrhage

This condition is also sometimes seen in horses working at high speeds. The horse bleeds from the blood vessels of the lungs during or after exercise at high speeds. This is relatively common in young racehorses, and is rarely severe, although occasionally cases are seen where a major blood vessel ruptures and a horse may bleed to death in this manner. Again, there is no real appropriate first aid, and nothing that can be done. The source of the bleeding may be identified by endoscopy, but there is little other than rest that can be helpful.

Worm-Related Damage

Potentially fatal bleeding in the lungs can occur through worm-related damage of the blood vessels. Larval stages of the strongyle worm can cause damage to the blood vessels, and aneurysms (bulges in the walls of blood vessels as a result of weakness at the site) may form. When subjected to high blood pressure, these aneurysms may rupture. Bleeding may be seen from the nose, or may be confined within the chest cavity.

Acute Allergic Airway Disease

Acute allergic airway disease is another cause of respiratory distress and difficulty breathing. Although not due to an injury as such, inhalation of allergens can cause acute inflammation within the lungs, which in turn can cause symptoms vary-

ing from heavy breathing and coughing to collapse with severe difficulty breathing and subsequent death. This is covered in Chapter 5.

Smoke Inhalation

Horses that have been in a fire often have skin injuries (see Chapter 8) as well as potentially having burns in the throat and lungs caused by the inhalation of hot smoke. Smoke inhalation can cause swelling of the affected areas and difficulty in breathing. In the longer term, it can cause significant irritation of the lungs, which can result in severe lung disease with breathing problems and, in some cases, loss of inflammatory fluid from the nose. This is particularly marked if smoke from burning plastics is inhaled.

The Heart

Injury to the heart is extremely uncommon, but penetrating foreign bodies occasionally (and catastrophically) cause damage to this organ.

Few other types of heart disease can be categorized as injury, although sometimes acute exacerbation of pre-existing heart conditions can occur through exercise or stress. This type of problem can sometimes be avoided by regular monitoring of the heart (e.g. at the time of yearly vaccinations). If a murmur (abnormal sound) or rhythm disturbance is picked up, future exercise levels can be reduced (see Chapter 5). If early signs of heart disease are not recognized, exercise-related stress can damage the heart further. This can result in sudden symptoms of heart disease, such as fatigue, breathlessness, coughing, swelling of the limbs, neck and belly, a weakened pulse, collapse (which can be extremely dangerous for a rider), and even death.

10 Abdominal Injuries

Injuries involving the abdomen and its constituent organs are thankfully rare. However, damage resulting from penetrating injuries can occur, and foaling difficulties can also cause injuries to the abdominal and pelvic organs. Wounds in the abdominal area may involve the skin only, or may also involve underlying structures (see Chapter 8). The muscular layer of tissue that lies beneath the skin is relatively thin in this area so penetrating injuries can potentially involve the abdominal cavity.

PERITONITIS

Inflammation or infection of the cavity that surrounds the abdominal organs (the peritoneal cavity) is referred to as peritonitis. This is a potentially lethal disease, which can result from infection or injury of either the organs within this cavity, or penetration of the cavity from outside.

The symptoms of peritonitis include lethargy, depression, high temperature, weight loss, inappetance, and colic. The abdominal muscles often become tense and take on a 'boarded' appearance. The depth and severity of any wounds therefore need to be carefully assessed so that, should penetration of the peritoneal cavity be present, they can be managed appropriately to avoid peritonitis developing.

RUPTURES AND HERNIAS

Hernias occur when the enlargement of a natural opening in the abdominal musculature enables abdominal contents to leave the abdominal cavity and come to lie under the skin, where they cause swelling. Typical hernia sites include the umbilicus (or belly button), the inguinal or groin opening, and the scrotal opening in the male. Pieces of abdominal fatty tissue, or even loops of gut, can become trapped; if the latter happens, severe and potentially fatal colic can result.

The commonest type of hernia is the umbilical hernia, which is usually seen in young foals. The connection between the abdominal cavity and the umbilical cord should shrink down within a few days of birth, but in some individuals an opening remains in the muscular layer, which allows abdominal contents to pass through and lie under the skin. Umbilical hernias in young foals should be monitored carefully. If they are small, any material protruding through the gap should be pushed back into the abdominal cavity on a daily basis. This can result in the gradual narrowing of the deficit, and reduce the potential for a serious hernia to occur. More serious hernias may require surgical correction at an early age. Scrotal and inguinal hernias are rare, but do occur,

Ruptures occur when a tear in the muscular wall of the abdominal cavity results in the development of a rent through which tissues can protrude. Such an opening occurs from trauma, and can be associated with lacerations to the skin. Swellings on the surface of the abdomen should be investigated by a vet to rule out such conditions because, should abdominal contents pass through such an opening, gut loops may become trapped, and colic can follow.

THE DIGESTIVE SYSTEM

The Abdominal Organs

Injury to the organs and viscerae of the gastro-intestinal tract (*see* Fig. 42) is rare. Direct damage to the liver (and the spleen – although this is not a digestive

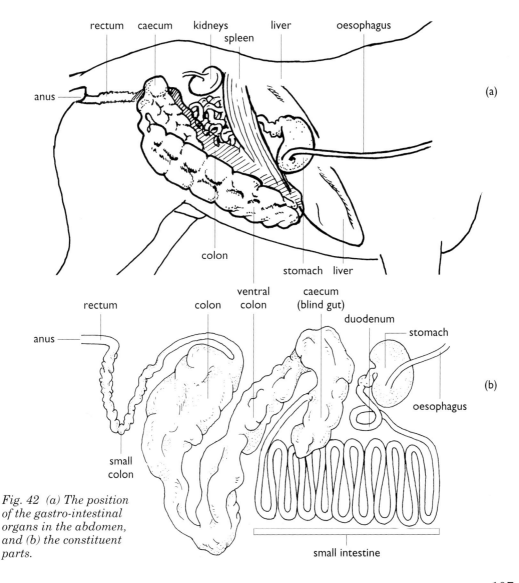

Fig. 42 (a) The position of the gastro-intestinal organs in the abdomen, and (b) the constituent parts.

107

organ) can result from high-velocity blunt trauma, and bruising or rupture can potentially occur. In the horse, however, these organs are largely protected by the back of the ribcage and so this type of injury is extremely rare. It is possible, though, for penetrating objects to damage these organs and cause severe bleeding.

The Guts

Damage to the guts can occur for a variety of reasons, such as worm damage (which can cause both direct injury of the gut walls as well as affecting their blood supply) and other causes of colic. Swelling of the guts from fermentation of food, or from the presence of a blockage (such as a twist), also causes direct damage to the gut walls, and catastrophic gut rupture can result.

Colic

The term colic technically means 'abdominal pain'. It therefore encompasses a variety of conditions of differing cause and severity, and is not, in itself, a diagnosis. There are many causes of colic in the horse, which can result in symptoms ranging from lack of appetite and a dull demeanour to thrashing, rolling, kicking, sweating and collapse. The precipitating cause of colic in a particular case is often difficult to determine. Early recognition of the severity of the disease is particularly important. Horses with colic should always be treated as an emergency, and it is important to seek veterinary attention as early as possible because cases of colic rarely get better on their own.

Whilst awaiting the vet it is a good idea to lead the horse round, both from the point of view of preventing him from rolling, and to help relieve internal spasm. However, contrary to popular belief, it is rare for rolling to cause twists

in the gut; for the most part these result from disturbances in gut motility.

A vet examining a horse with colic will first assess whether the problem is likely to be one that requires an operation. Such cases would be those where a twist is present in the gut, or where there is some other serious blockage or loss of blood supply to part of the intestines.

Determination of the source of pain is based on a thorough clinical examination, some aspects of which can be monitored by the owner whilst awaiting the vet (see Chapter 2). The pulse rate of the horse is probably the most accurate indicator of severity of pain; for the most part cases of mild colic have pulse rates in the range of 30–50 beats per minute, and those requiring surgery often have pulse rates in excess of 60. Examination of the colour of the gums gives information about the circulation. Horses that are very ill, and may have gut twists, often have brick-red or dull-brownish gums due to release of bacterial toxins into the bloodstream. Presence or absence of gut noise is also helpful; the horse that has active guts and is passing dung is less at risk than one with reduced gut motility.

Your vet will usually carry out a rectal examination, which can give information both about gut motility and whether or not there is abnormal positioning of internal organs consistent with, for instance, a twist. Your vet may also need to pass a stomach tube via the nostril (this can cause a nosebleed) into the stomach. Twists and consequent blockage can result in the build-up of fluid in the stomach, which can be removed by stomach tube; it can also be useful to give some medication via stomach tube.

Mild Colic
Mild pain occurs, in most cases, with either spasm or tympany (gas build-up). Approximately 70 per cent of spasmodic colics are caused by worms. These result either from

the movement of worms within or through the guts, or from the sudden death of large numbers of worms in a heavily infested horse that has recently been wormed. Rectal examination confirms the presence of spasm, and these cases often respond well to mild painkillers and antispasmodic medication.

Tympanitic or flatulent colic may result from digestive disturbances that result in fermentation. This can follow the feeding of foods with a high sugar content, such as spring grass, good-quality hay, or high-energy short feeds. The resultant gas often causes swelling of the abdomen as well as flatulence. Build-up of gas can cause twists, or partial twists can cause the build-up of gas. The use of relatively strong painkillers is often necessary, and in some cases surgical decompression may be required.

Mild cases of colic can also result from changes in weather, travelling, stress and dietary change.

More Severe Colic

More severe colic can result from the progression of mild colic without or despite treatment. Pain and an interruption in normal gut motility, for whatever reason, can lead to twists. Where there is a twisted gut the blood supply to a section of gut is removed, causing intense pain. The subsequent death of the affected piece of bowel can result in the release of naturally occurring bacteria and toxins from the bowel into the bloodstream, leading to the development of septicaemia and toxaemia, which can be fatal. Gut rupture can also occur.

Similar signs are seen where the blood supply to a section of bowel is disrupted by movement of strongyle worms, or where a section of bowel becomes blocked by an internal tumour. In all such cases surgery is required, and in most cases it is necessary to remove the affected section of bowel. Grass sickness can cause colic that appears to be due to a twisted small intestine, because the disruption in gut motility that it causes can result in severe pain and distended small bowel. It may not be possible to diagnose grass sickness without surgery, but where it is diagnosed euthanasia is usually necessary.

Other obstructions that can cause colic include impactions (blockages) that usually follow the overeating of roughage or the swallowing of large quantities of earth (sand colic) whilst grazing short grass. Impactions can often be felt whilst examining rectally, and may respond well to pain relief and laxatives by stomach tube or in food. They can sometimes take several days to clear and in some cases hospitalisation may be necessary for intensive care. Surgery is rarely required. A useful tip to monitor whether your horse is eating earth or sand is to mix some dung with water and see if sand settles out.

By far the majority of cases of colic seen respond to treatment given by the vet on the first visit and make rapid recoveries.

Some cases of mild colic do recur as the pain-relieving medication wears off, and may need further treatment. Those cases that need to be referred to an equine hospital are in the minority, but where diagnosis of a condition requiring surgery is made, or where colic is seen despite the use of pain relief, referral becomes necessary. Equine hospitals have diagnostic techniques at their disposal that the average vet in practice does not have access to, as well as intensive-care and surgical facilities.

Gut Rupture

As well as potentially resulting from some forms of colic, gut rupture can also occur following wounds, and damage to the hindgut can occur during mating, foaling, or even rectal examination. Complete rupture of the guts with spillage of gut contents is not treatable.

Rectal Tears

Rectal tears often involve only partial-thickness injuries of the gut wall, and with careful management these can heal. Affected horses show signs including depression, inappetance, straining, and colic. Peritonitis can easily occur. Veterinary assessment, first aid and prompt hospitalisation for further treatment is of paramount importance for recovery. Rectal tears are classified according to the depth of the rent in the rectal wall, and their treatment depends on this. Treatment is aimed at allowing healing, and preventing faecal contamination of the peritoneal cavity by starving the horse, removing faeces, packing the area, and administering anti-inflammatories, antibiotics, and medication to reduce straining.

Rectal Prolapse

Rectal prolapse can be seen in horses, although it is very rare. A portion of the rectum can be seen protruding from the anus. It can be caused by excessive straining due to other diseases such as diarrhoea, constipation, the presence of rectal tears (see above) and also foaling. These cases are also emergencies, and there is no effective first aid, other than to prevent the horse from rubbing the prolapsed section of bowel and damaging it. Treatment includes manual reduction of the prolapse and medical treatment with anti-inflammatories, antibiotics and drugs to reduce straining where possible; surgical resection or even euthanasia may be necessary in severe cases.

THE URINARY SYSTEM

Damage to the urinary system is rare. However, there is a number of conditions that may affect the system.

Bladder Rupture

Bladder rupture is particularly common in newborn foals. Male Thoroughbred foals are particularly at risk. The condition occurs when the pressure exerted on a full bladder during the birth process causes leakage of urine into the peritoneum. A foal affected by this will show symptoms that include depression, inappetance, colic, and straining. A reduced output of urine may also be seen since the urine leaks into the peritoneal cavity rather than being passed out normally. These symptoms may easily be confused, however, with retained meconium (constipation with birth faeces). Early recognition with surgical treatment can be successful. Otherwise, these foals die.

Bladder rupture can occasionally also be seen in adult horses. It can follow a foaling injury – if one of the foal's legs penetrates the wall of the bladder – but more often it occurs due to blockage of the urethra (the tube from the bladder to the outside) with crystals or bladder stones. In these cases, severe abdominal pain accompanied by lack of urination is a symptom that persists for some time before bladder rupture occurs.

Bladder Prolapse

Bladder prolapse or eversion can follow difficult foaling. Abnormal contraction of bruised or damaged organs in the abdomen and pelvis can result in their appearance from the anus or vulva. If the bladder prolapses, it appears in this area as a pale pink, smooth bag containing urine. For this to occur, it must prolapse via a full-thickness tear in the vagina or rectum. Urination is prevented, and signs of abdominal pain, straining and distress are seen. These cases are surgical emergencies if they are to have a chance of recovery.

Bladder Eversion

Bladder eversion can occur if the bladder turns itself inside out and prolapses via the urethra to appear from the vulva. It has a roughish red appearance, and urine may be seen to drip from its surface. This is also an emergency, and is likely to require surgery.

THE REPRODUCTIVE SYSTEM IN THE MARE

Vaginal Injury

Although vaginal injuries can be caused by kicks, injuries to the reproductive system of the mare (see Fig. 43) occur most often at mating or foaling. Difficult foalings can result in the foal causing bruising or rupture of adjacent tissues with a foot as he passes through the birth canal. Sometimes stallions penetrate the rectum

rather than the vagina on mating, and rectal bruising or rectal tears can result (see page 110). Vaginal bruising is not uncommon, and may require no treatment. Some older mares have varicose veins in the vagina and these may become damaged and may bleed during mating or foaling. Occasionally, they may also bleed spontaneously in late pregnancy, which can be mistaken for early signs of foaling. Bleeding from the varicose veins rarely requires treatment.

Vaginal tears can occur during mating or foaling, and can potentially cause sequelae. These range from the formation of adhesions within the vagina, which can complicate foaling and prevent future conception, to the development of peritonitis (see page 106). Other complications at foaling include damage to the cervix, the womb itself, and even the rectum or bladder. Vaginal tears can involve the tissue that separates the vagina from the

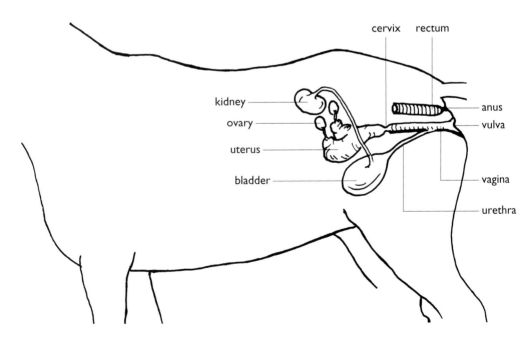

Fig. 43 The female urino-genital tract.

rectum, and formation of a fistula with passage of some faeces via the vulva is a possibility. This obviously requires surgical treatment, and can cause infertility.

Vulval Tears

Vulval tears are a common sequel to many foalings. Mares suffer little discomfort from slight tears to the lips of the vulva. These should be attended to, however, since if they are not sutured correctly the vulval seal may be lost, resulting in future contamination of the vagina with faeces, which can cause infertility. If the vulva is not stitched within a few hours of birth, the optimum time for suturing the vulva is four to six weeks later when all the inflammation has abated. In some cases the edges of the tear may simply be re-aligned. In many, a 'Caslick's' operation (partial suturing of the lips of the vulva) is carried out. This is also used to prevent infertility in mares whose poor vulval conformation makes the vagina susceptible to faecal contamination. Urination and mating are possible via the gap that remains, but the vulva must be reopened before foaling or more serious vulval tears will result.

Cervical and Uterine Injury

Cervical and uterine tears result in excessive blood loss at the time of foaling. Depending on their depth, peritonitis may be a risk, but a more common result is future infertility owing to the damaged cervix no longer forming an effective seal.

Another possible consequence of a difficult foaling (although it can also occur in heavily pregnant mares subjected to excessive exercise) is rupture of the middle uterine artery, which feeds the womb. This causes major blood loss, which may either pass into the abdominal cavity and not be seen, or be lost from the vulva, or be contained within the artery's ligament causing a massive and painful blood blister. In the first two cases, the blood loss is not preventable, and most mares bleed to death within a few hours. In the latter case blood loss can be sufficient to cause death, but severe colic with depression and weakness can also be seen. Some of these mares will survive with appropriate supportive treatment.

Prolapse of the Uterus
Prolapse of the uterus occurs occasionally following a difficult foaling. The uterus is seen protuding from the vagina as a massive red bag of tissue. Rupture of the middle uterine artery is a further complication in many cases, but whether or not this is present, these mares rarely survive the overwhelming shock of such an injury.

Pregnancy in the older mare

Some older mares in particular suffer from loss of the muscular support to the abdomen in late pregnancy, and are seen to have a 'dropped' appearance. This can prevent normal muscular contractions from being sufficiently strong, and may necessitate assistance at foaling.

FOALING

Foaling is always a potential emergency. Assistance at foaling should always be provided for any mare that has strained for more than 30 minutes without result. It is advisable to call the vet at this stage so that help can be given if necessary, although in most cases this simple precaution guarantees a normal delivery by the time the vet arrives!

Fig. 44 The result of a successful foaling.

If a mare is in serious difficulties, she may be assisted. First check that the foal is arriving in the correct position – a head and two front legs should be presented. If not, the foal may need to be turned within the womb before it can be delivered, so pulling on it is not to be advised. If the head and front legs are presented, they can be grasped by hand, and gentle traction can be provided to help the mare each time she pushes.

Premature Separation of the Placental Membranes

Another potential problem can be recognized by seeing the presentation of the foal within a bag that is red rather than pale pink on the outside. This indicates premature separation of the placental membranes, which causes the foal to be in distress. The foal must be born quickly if it is to live.

Retention of the Placental Membranes

Retention of the afterbirth (which in horses is normally passed within four hours of birth) can cause potentially fatal endotoxaemia and overwhelming infection if left untreated. Similar problems can result if even a small section of the afterbirth is left within, so the afterbirth should always be spread out and examined to ensure that no pieces are missing. For this reason (the potential for tearing of the afterbirth and, in fact, the lining of the womb), pulling on the protruding section of a partially retained afterbirth is also contra-indicated. Instead, veterinary treatment must be sought within six hours of birth.

THE REPRODUCTIVE SYSTEM IN THE STALLION

Testicular Damage and Injury

Damage to the scrotum, and testicular trauma, can result from kick injuries as well as from direct damage such as that sustained when falling over jumps. Inflammation and pain are seen in the acute phase, often with marked swelling.

113

Resulting infection can cause subsequent infertility.

Testicular torsion is an uncommon disease in which one of the testicles becomes twisted on its axis. This can cause similar symptoms to testicular trauma, but may require surgical treatment. Similar signs may also be caused by scrotal hernias (*see* page 106). If a loop of gut comes to reside in the scrotal sac it can become trapped, and severe colic requiring surgery can be necessary. Any cause of scrotal swelling with associated pain should therefore be investigated promptly by a vet.

Damage to the Penis

Damage to the penis can be caused by kick injuries, especially during attempts to mate. Occasionally, mating can cause inflammation of the penis which can result in difficulty urinating afterwards,

and traces of blood may be seen in the urine. This rarely requires treatment, but should be investigated.

Sustained Erection
Sustained erection, or 'priapism', can occur, whether or not mating has taken place. It can be complicated by swelling of the penis, which can prevent its being withdrawn into the prepuce. A vicious circle can be set up where ongoing inflammation and fluid retention causes more inability to withdraw, and pressure of the erect penis on the nerves that supply it can prevent it receiving the nerve impulses that allow it to withdraw. This can result in permanent damage to the penis. Surgical treatment to replace the penis in the prepuce may be needed, or the penis may need to be strapped up to the body-wall to prevent further damage whilst treatment to reduce inflammation is initiated.

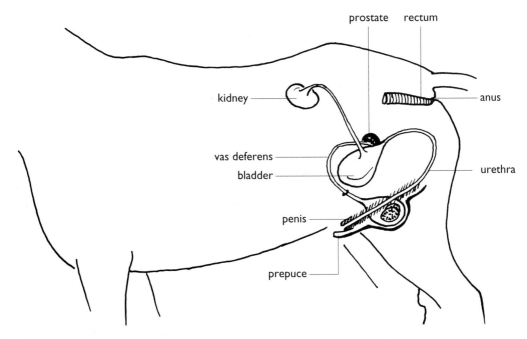

Fig. 45 The male urino-genital tract.

11 Lameness

Lameness is one of the commonest causes of the inability of horses to work. In some cases, it is avoidable. However, given the shape of the horse's skeleton, and the variety of athletic feats we expect of our horses, it is surprising that they do not suffer from lameness more often. Although lameness commonly occurs as a catastrophic event, whether when working, or when turned out at grass, in many cases that catastrophic event is the culmination of underlying stresses and strains, which may have been avoidable. In other cases, lameness develops gradually, and it is hard to pinpoint the cause.

Every time a horse's leg makes contact with the ground the force of impact is transmitted up from the weight-bearing parts of the hoof through the bones and joints of the limb. The force increases with the speed at which the leg meets the ground and with the hardness of the ground; where the ground is firm, less strain is dissipated on impact. When a horse lands from a jump, the first leg to touch the ground bears, for an instant, the full weight of horse, tack and rider. Shock absorption is for the most part transferred to the digital cushion through the contact of the frog with the ground, and to the tendons and ligaments via the fluid within the joints. Damage to the limb can take many forms, but it is most likely to occur in horses whose conformation and/or strength and fitness of limb or foot is less than ideal, and especially likely when these factors are combined with hard ground.

AVOIDING LAMENESS

The avoidance of injuries causing lameness may, in some cases, be possible with exemplary care, good foot balance, and the maintenance of a suitable state of fitness. And whilst even the best of care will not prevent lameness caused by external injuries, the conformation and balance of the horse, as well as his ability to perform at the level required, should be taken into account when determining the preventative measures that may be taken.

Limb Conformation

Horses with poor conformation may never be capable of performing at the same level as those with better conformation.

In horses with poor limb conformation, abnormal stresses will pass through the limbs, so predisposing them to injury. Similarly, horses with abnormal back conformation are more likely to suffer from back problems. In the perfect limb, a straight line dropped from the shoulder or hip, and perpendicular to the ground, should pass through the centre of the joints and down through the centre of the foot (see Figs 7–8). This line represents the direction of the force exerted by the weight of the horse, so it must be perpendicular and central in order to distribute the horse's weight evenly through the joints.

A horse whose toes turn in may bear excessive strains through the outside of the limb, which may in turn increase the likelihood of problems in the joints. A horse that is back at the knee is likely to have increased strains in the flexor tendons, and is thus more at risk of straining or tearing a tendon, particularly where this stress is increased by concussion. Similarly, a horse that is knock-kneed or 'cow-hocked' (whose hocks turn in) will necessarily have abnormal strains passing through the bones and joints, and may be more likely to have problems in these joints. This makes them more liable to damage such as stress fractures, arthritic change and, to a lesser extent, tendon and ligament injuries.

The angle of the feet in relation to the higher joints is also significant. The angle of the front of the foot should ideally equal the angle of the pastern from the side, so an imaginary straight line should pass from the centre of the fetlock joint through the pastern and coffin joints to the centre of the hoof (see Fig. 9). This is called the hoof–pastern axis. The angle between the heel and the ground should equal that made between the toe and the ground; the heels and the toe should thus be parallel. From the front or back, the angle and length of the side walls of the hoof should be equal, the width of the hoof should equal the length from the point of the toe to each side of the base of the frog, and, in the perfect horse, the coronary band should be parallel to the ground.

Like the horse that is back at the knee, the one that is tipped onto his heels, with low or collapsed heels and long toes, has increased stresses placed on his flexor tendons and sesamoid bones, which may predispose them to injury. A long toe and collapsed heels can also cause excessive forces to be applied to the navicular bone and, together with low-grade concussion, can predispose the horse to navicular syndrome as well as corns (see Fig. 14). Concussion leads to inflammation within the hoof, which can predispose the navicular

bone to disease, particularly where abnormal conformation increases the strain through the deep digital flexor tendon, which runs over the navicular bone (see Figs 46 and 48).

In horses with very upright foot conformation, shock absorption is inadequate, and concussion is increased, potentially causing more inflammation within the hoof capsule, and higher in the limb. Such a horse will be more susceptible to the development of arthritis and ringbone.

Poor foot shape and poor foot balance can be the result of disease rather than natural conformation. Low-grade, chronic lameness in a single limb typically results in the foot on that limb developing, over time, a rather boxy, upright shape. This is because that limb will bear less weight than its opposite counterpart. Chronic laminitis leads to the development of long toes and low heels, because in order to avoid pain the horse is constantly trying to take his weight off his toes. In horses with severe laminitis, the pedal bone can rotate downwards within the foot (see laminitis, pages 123–8), leading to a curving of the front wall of the hoof, and a dropped sole.

General conformation is discussed in detail in Chapter 1.

Foot Balance

Foot balance also has a significant effect on the horse's ability to perform. The feet should be trimmed and, where necessary, reshod every four to six weeks. However, even with regular farriery a foot may be poorly balanced, and this will inevitably place abnormal stress on the limbs. Corrective farriery, on the other hand, can go a long way to normalizing the stresses passed through the limbs of a horse with poor conformation.

The foot should be trimmed to optimize the hoof–pastern axis by cutting back the toe where necessary and trimming the toe and the heels appropriately. If the toes are left too long, break-over will be impaired, and the horse may develop a tendency to break over the limb to the side, which can contribute to a dishing type of gait.

In addition, the side walls of the hoof should be trimmed so that the weight-bearing surface of the hoof is perpendicular to the weight-bearing axis of the lower limb. This can be assessed by lifting the limb and using a T-bar to examine this area (although a trained eye will be able to assess it merely by sight), or by watching the horse when walked and trotted in a straight line on a firm surface, and paying attention to the way each foot lands: check that each lands square – that both the outer and inner edge of the foot makes contact with the ground at the same time, and not one before the other.

The shoe should be placed to support both sides of the foot as well as the back and the front. Support to the heels as well as to the toe is important. It is common to see shoes applied to the weight-bearing part of the hoof only; and, especially on horses with long toes and contracted heels, this can mean that the front of the foot is bearing all the weight, which can lead to further problems. Such foot conformation requires the bars of the shoe to extend beyond the weight-bearing part of the hoof, thus giving support to the heels and encouraging them to spread back.

The unbalanced foot that is poorly or unevenly trimmed can pass abnormal stress to the joints, and insufficient trimming can cause the loss of proper contact between the frog and the ground, which reduces shock absorption. Insufficient trimming or poor shoeing can also predispose the hoof to splaying, which leads to sand cracks. In the badly shod horse it may be found either that he no longer bears weight evenly across the hoof, or that the weight is brought to bear on the sole (particularly if the sole is less than concave) as well as on the hoof wall, predisposing the soles to bruising. Direct concussive damage to the soles makes the pedal bone susceptible to damage. Assymetrical wear on a shoe may indicate poor foot balance.

Fitness

Given that the foot balance is as good as it can be, the other area where work can be done to avoid injury is in the build-up and maintenance of a suitable level of fitness. This should start with the young horse, for whom a sensible regime of work should be initiated according to his capabilities. To expect a young horse to perform at a high level is to court problems. Equally, with advancing age, horses become less able to attain and maintain a high level of strength and fitness, and may not be capable of the standard of performance they attained when younger.

Fitness does not just relate to a horse's capability to work without getting tired. During an ascending regime of work, stress adaptation occurs within the bones and soft tissues, which allows them to strengthen in keeping with the work being done. Horses are very willing creatures, and will generally attempt to work if asked to do so. Ask a horse to, for instance, jump a cross-country course when he has not been working at speed or over fences recently, and he will probably do his best. However, even if he does not seem to be having difficulty, the structures of his limbs will be subjected to stresses that they may be unable to cope with. In addition, horses that are not properly fit become tired, and it is when they are pushing themselves to the limit that they are more likely to put a foot wrong and fall, crash into a fence, or even suffer a catastrophic event like a tendon injury by subjecting a tendon that is already at its limit of elasticity to further stress. It is vitally important, therefore, that horses develop and maintain the level of fitness they need for the work that they are going to do. If you are unable to exercise a horse all week, but then ask him to perform at the weekend, you create a situation in which the likelihood of injury is greatly increased.

The Going

Any concussion-related injuries are obviously more likely to occur when a horse is working on hard ground. Typically, such injuries (for instance, fracture of the pedal bone, navicular bone, cannon bone, etc.) occur in immature animals on the racecourse, but occasionally stress fractures are seen in event horses. Other acute injuries that are more common where the ground is hard include damage to the tendons or suspensory ligament.

On the other hand, working on ground that is too soft commonly results in joint and muscle strain. This is because soft going increases the chances of the horse's placing his feet in an unbalanced manner and slipping.

RECOGNIZING LAMENESS

Although lamenesses may be recognizable from the saddle as limping or stride imbalance, they are best assessed by trotting the horse up on firm, even ground, both in a straight line and on a circle. When doing this, the horse should be allowed a loose rein, so that his natural head movements can be observed.

In most cases, a forelimb lameness will manifest itself in head nodding: as the weight is borne on the sore leg, the horse tenses his forequarters in an attempt to reduce the weight borne on that leg, and this causes the head to rise up; then, as the

sound leg bears weight, the muscles relax and the head nods down.

Hindlimb lamenesses can be more difficult to assess as there is usually no head nodding. Instead, the hindquarters tense and lift as the weight is borne on the painful leg, and drop as the sound leg bears weight. The lame leg typically bears less of the horse's weight (and for a shorter period) than the contra-lateral leg. This can be assessed by ear because on concrete the lame foot makes a quieter and 'shorter' noise than the sound leg. In addition, some types of lameness cause the height of the foot's flight to be reduced, and this can be appreciated by watching carefully.

Bilateral lamenesses (those affecting both limbs) are more difficult to appreciate. Often the affected horse appears to be more 'pottery' than lame, but lungeing on a circle can often aid appreciation of these cases, as the leg on the inside of the circle often then appears to be the lamest.

Grading Lameness

To aid assessment, and to assist in monitoring improvement or deterioration, lameness is graded according to its severity. Some vets ascribe grades between 1 and 5, others between 1 and 10; the latter range allows more detailed assessment.

Grade 5/5 (or 10/10) defines a lameness in which the horse is unable to bear weight on the affected limb. In many cases these horses are suffering from fractures. A horse that is 9/10 lame may be able to touch the toe to the ground, but no more; this may be caused by septic arthritis, subsolar abcess or a very severe tendonitis. One that is 4/5 or 8/10 shows obvious hobbling lameness at a walk. Grade 3/5 or 6/10 is less severe than the above, but is nevertheless easily detectable, causing a head nod at walk, and a hobbling gait if trot is attempted. Grade 2/5 or 4/10 can easily be seen at a trot (some degree of a head nod may be seen), but is barely detectable at walk; grade 1/5 or 2/10 is barely detectable even at a trot, and there is no head nod. Grade 0 defines a horse that is sound.

Grading the severity of lameness

Grade 0	Sound.
Grade 2/10	Barely detectable lameness at walk and trot.
Grade 4/10	Barely detectable lameness at walk; easily detectable at trot.
Grade 6/10	Easily detectable lameness at walk.
Grade 8/10	Hobbling at walk; inability or unwillingness to trot.
Grade 10/10	Complete – non-weight-bearing – lameness.

EXAMINING THE LAME HORSE

Clinical examination of a lame horse includes assessment of the cardiovascular and respiratory systems (see Chapter 2) as well as manual investigation of the back, neck and limbs. The limbs are felt from top to bottom (see Fig. 46 for underlying structures), and any signs of heat, pain, swelling or other abnormality is noted. All joints are manipulated, and the foot is picked out fully and cleaned before a hoof-tester is used to apply pressure across the foot to assess for pain. If the foot is painful, it is likely that the shoes will need to be removed in order to permit a full solar examination. This may have to be followed up with paring of the foot with a hoof knife.

Making a Diagnosis

If clinical examination of the horse, manipulation and palpation of all the limbs, and trotting the horse up is not sufficient to identify the source of pain and allow a diagnosis to be made, a variety of further techniques can be employed.

Flexion Tests
Flexion tests work by exacerbating low-grade joint problems, so aiding diagnosis, but their reliability has been disputed by some practitioners. The test involves holding up the limb in a flexed position for approximately one minute, and then trotting the horse straight off on firm, level ground. Although many horses will appear lame for the first few strides, those that continue to limp are assessed as positive to the test, which may indicate an underlying joint problem such as arthritis.

Nerve Blocks
Nerve blocks are extremely useful because they allow specific nerves or joints in the limb to be isolated, so preventing them from receiving the normal pain signals. The skin over the nerve is first clipped and cleaned, and then a small amount of local anaesthetic is injected next to the nerve or into the joint. After some minutes, the effectiveness of the block is tested (for instance by pricking the skin in the area and seeing if this results in a reflex withdrawal of the limb), and the horse is trotted up again. If the grade of lameness is reduced, or if the horse becomes sound, the source of pain has been identified.

X-rays
If bone or joint problems are suspected, X-rays (radiographs) of the area can be taken. However, it may be necessary to take a number of images from slightly

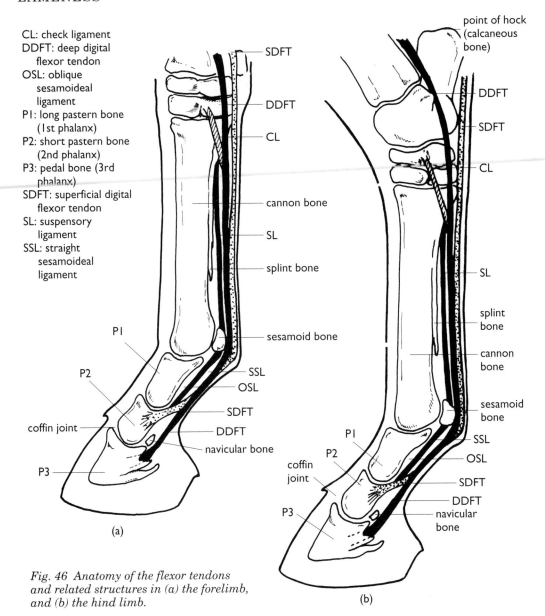

CL: check ligament
DDFT: deep digital
    flexor tendon
OSL: oblique
    sesamoideal
    ligament
PI: long pastern bone
    (1st phalanx)
P2: short pastern bone
    (2nd phalanx)
P3: pedal bone (3rd
    phalanx)
SDFT: superficial digital
    flexor tendon
SL: suspensory
    ligament
SSL: straight
    sesamoideal
    ligament

*Fig. 46 Anatomy of the flexor tendons
and related structures in (a) the forelimb,
and (b) the hind limb.*

different angles as small areas of bony abnormality can easily be hidden by over-lying bone, and may only be seen when one particular image happens to bring it within view. Extensive bony abnormalities, such as severe arthritis, are often easy to see, even with only a few views.

Portable X-ray machines are very useful when it is necessary to X-ray the horse on site, but the best results are usually obtained by taking your horse to the vet. This allows immediate processing of the radiographs, which means that further images can immediately be taken if the

120

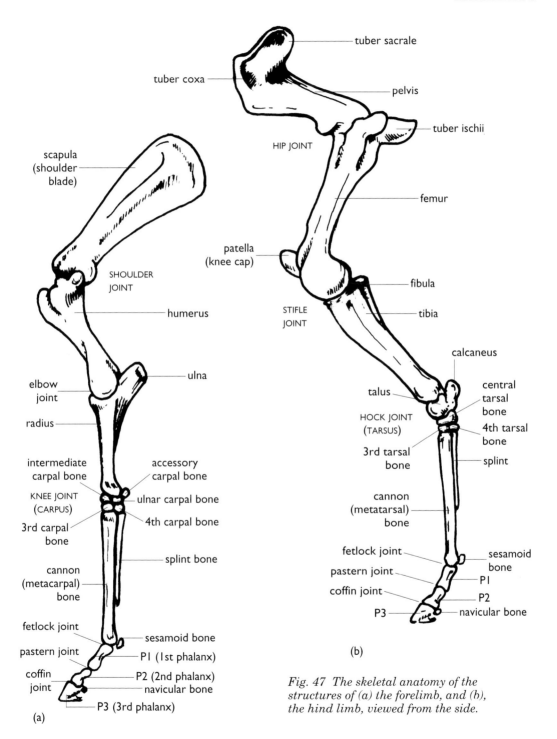

tuber sacrale

tuber coxa

pelvis

tuber ischii

HIP JOINT

scapula
(shoulder
blade)

femur

SHOULDER
JOINT

patella
(knee cap)

humerus

STIFLE
JOINT

fibula

tibia

elbow
joint

ulna

calcaneus

talus

central
tarsal
bone

HOCK JOINT
(TARSUS)

4th tarsal
bone

radius

3rd tarsal
bone

splint

intermediate
carpal bone

accessory
carpal bone

KNEE JOINT
(CARPUS)

ulnar carpal bone

cannon
(metatarsal)
bone

3rd carpal
bone

4th carpal bone

splint bone

fetlock joint

sesamoid
bone

cannon
(metacarpal)
bone

pastern joint

PI

coffin joint

P2

fetlock joint

sesamoid bone

P3

navicular bone

pastern joint

PI (1st phalanx)

(b)

coffin
joint

P2 (2nd phalanx)
navicular bone

Fig. 47 The skeletal anatomy of the
structures of (a) the forelimb, and (b),
the hind limb, viewed from the side.

P3 (3rd phalanx)

(a)

initial ones do not reveal anything. If you wish to hold your horse whilst X-rays are being taken, your vet will give you protective garments to wear. If there is any chance that you might be pregnant, you should not be present. Children under 16 years should also not be present.

Ultrasound
Ultrasound imaging is very useful for examining soft tissue because it allows a live, moving image to be seen. It works because different types of tissue reflect or absorb sound to different degrees. The probe on an ultrasound scanner emits beams of sound, which travel into, and back from, the tissue being imaged. The returning sound pulses are measured, and used by the machine to create an instantaneous screen image of a 'slice' through the object. By moving the probe in different directions, different slices can be examined. For the most part these are either transverse images (images parallel to the ground) or longitudinal images (images perpendicular to the ground).

Ultrasonography can be used for a variety of problems, but is particularly useful in the assessment and monitoring of tendon injuries (*see* pages 142–6).

Nuclear Scintigraphy
Nuclear scintigraphy – used regularly at referral centres – is a very useful technique for finding the sites of inflammation and pain in some horses. It involves injecting the horse with a non-toxic radioactive liquid, which is then taken up from the blood vessels by cells in the body that are actively dividing. A probe that detects radioactivity is used to measure the levels of radiation in different areas. Areas in which there is inflammation, and thus more actively dividing cells, have higher levels of radiation and can therefore be identified.

COMMON CAUSES OF LAMENESS

Conditions of the Feet

Subsolar Abscess
Pus in the foot, or subsolar abscess, is the commonest cause of acute equine lameness. Many cases follow solar punctures that are sustained from treading on flints, nails and other sharp objects, but in some cases the cause is never known. If the offending item is still present in the foot, urgent veterinary attention should be sought. The foreign body should not be removed (if possible) until the vet arrives. This can allow the vet to examine the item, and possibly even X-ray it, in position, thus allowing for a better assessment of the likelihood of involvement of deeper structures.

Infection of the foot following a prick injury sustained during shoeing (*see* box opposite) causes progressive lameness that is usually apparent within 12 to 24 hours of shoeing. During this time bacteria are building up and forming pus under the sole, when some heat may be felt in the foot, and there may be an increased digital pulse (*see* Chapter 2) caused by the inflammation. The horse typically stands with the infected foot pointed out in front of him in an attempt to relieve pressure on the foot, which is usually so sore that the horse hobbles very obviously, even at a walk. As the disease progresses, the fetlock and pastern will become swollen.

It is usually necessary to remove the shoes so that the foot can be pared with a hoof knife to allow release of the pus. A nerve block (*see* page 119) is not usually necessary from a diagnostic point of view, but it can be helpful in controlling pain while the foot is pared. In some cases, the pus is released under pressure; in others, the oozing of some fluid is all that is seen. However, achieving effective drainage of the infection is of paramount importance, because, although antibiotics may help, the improvement will not be sustained if pus continues to build up.

Tubbing of the foot (for ten minutes twice daily in warm salty water) and/or poulticing (see Chapter 4) is necessary. Animalintex soaked in hot water should be applied to the pared area and bandaged on twice daily. An Equiboot helps to keep the poultice in place and the foot clean. In addition, antibiotics may be necessary, anti-tetanus medication should be given (particularly to those horses that have not recently been vaccinated), and anti-inflammatory painkillers may be prescribed for horses that are particularly uncomfortable. Poulticing should continue until the foot is cool and comfortable, and no further pus has been seen for two or three days. The foot should be kept clean and covered until granulation of the drainage hole has occurred.

Nail-prick injuries

However careful a farrier is whilst shoeing horses, nail pricks can easily occur. If the white line is penetrated (see Fig. 48), a nail prick may simply result in pain that can be relieved by removal of the shoe, but if the nail's penetration allows entry of bacteria an abscess can result.

Nail-prick injuries are most common in horses with poor hoof-horn quality, that is those whose hoof wall is thin and has a tendency to chip and flake. A food supplement containing biotin helps to improve horn quality and thus helps to avoid the problems associated with nail pricks. For horses that have particularly bad hooves, stick-on (nailless) shoes can be helpful.

Bruised Soles, Subsolar Haematoma and Corns

Bruised soles or subsolar haematomas often, but not always, cause lameness. They result from the sole of the foot being brought into weight-bearing contact with the ground. Horses whose soles are not particularly concave (i.e. they have flat feet or dropped soles), or whose feet are trimmed too short, are most susceptible. Bruised soles can also result from work on stony ground, or may even be caused by poor shoe fit. Where the shoes cause trauma at the angle between the wall and the bar of the foot at the heel, bruising is referred to as a corn. Corns usually follow the wearing of shoes that are too small, or shoes are left on too long. Horses with flat feet are also more prone to corns.

In some cases, paring of bruised tissue is necessary to release pressure and allow healing to occur. If bacteria colonize the inflamed area, an abscess can result (see page 122). Shoes need to be removed, and reshoeing should be carried out with extreme care. The use of a wide-webbed seated-out shoe is usually helpful as it will allow good distribution of pressure away from the area. In addition, anti-inflammatories may be needed to relieve pain.

Pedal Osteitis

Pedal osteitis (or ostitis) is an inflammatory disease of the pedal bone caused by concussion or bruising to the soles. It may present with signs of severe pain, and so may be confused with laminitis. Diagnosis rests on localization of pain with nerve blocks; and X-rays may show roughening of the border of the pedal bone, and areas of irregularity with new bone formation.

Laminitis

As the name suggests (lamin, from laminae; itis, meaning inflammation), this condition is inflammation of the laminae in the hoof. The laminae are the interlocking leaves of tissue that bond the hoof capsule to the surface of the pedal bone (see Fig. 48). This bond transmits the

123

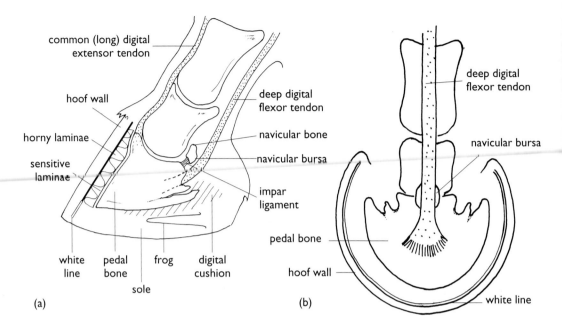

Fig. 48 Representation of the structures of the foot in cross-section, from the side (a), and from beneath (b).

weight of the horse from the skeleton to the hoof wall.

Inflammation (usually caused by an overload of carbohydrates in the diet, or by concussion, or by infection elsewhere in the system) disrupts the blood supply to the feet. This results in an increase in blood pressure at the same time as the blood supply to the sensitive laminae (*see* Fig. 48) is reduced; thus the laminae are starved of the nutrients that are essential in keeping them healthy. The consequent damage to the laminae, and fluid leakage from the blood vessels into the areas between them, weakens the bond between the sensitive and insensitive (horny) laminae. Combined with the tension that the deep digital flexor tendon exerts on the back of the pedal bone, this weakening of the laminar bonds allows the tip of the pedal bone to rotate downwards. And as more and more laminar bonds are lost, the laminae become less and less able to transfer the weight of the horse from the pedal bone to the hoof wall; the pedal bone may then begin to sink down within the foot. Eventually the pedal bone may come to press on the sole, causing it to bulge; in very advanced cases, it may even penetrate the sole completely.

Laminitis is extremely painful, causing initial symptoms of bilateral (usually) forelimb lameness with a shortened 'pottery' gait. On examination, the feet are typically found to be warm, and to have an increased pulse in the digital arteries (*see* Chapter 2), which indicates the presence of inflammation in this area. In severe cases the horse tends to lean back, trying to take his weight on his heels (since pain is generally most intense in the toe area), and is often seen to shift his weight constantly from one side to the other. The horse may be reluctant to move, particularly in cases where the hind limbs are also affected, and he may even be reluctant to stand.

When you suspect laminitis, it is important to isolate the horse from food and to avoid any exercise (and thus concussion). Then seek prompt veterinary attention because even apparently mild cases can quickly progress to become severe. In most cases, box-rest and a reduced diet (total starvation can lead to more serious problems) are necessary initially. If very recent overeating of carbohydrates is the cause of the condition, it may be necessary to stomach-tube the horse with mineral oil to clear the system and prevent further carbohydrate absorption.

Medication with bute (phenylbutazone) and other anti-inflammatory drugs (see Appendix) can help to limit the inflammation and make the animal more comfortable. Drugs that lower the blood pressure, and thus reduce fluid leakage between the laminae, are also widely used. Examples of these include ACP (acepromazine), isoxsuprine hydrochloride and phenoxybenzamine hydrochloride.

Support to the frog helps prevent further injury (see Fig. 49), and in acute cases a bandaged-on frog support may be used. Heart-bar shoes also give support to the frogs but they should not be fitted until X-rays have revealed the precise position of the pedal bone within the foot. If there is rotation of the pedal bone it may also be necessary for the farrier to rebalance the foot by cutting back the dorsal wall of the hoof to realign it with the pedal bone before shoes are fitted (see Fig. 50).

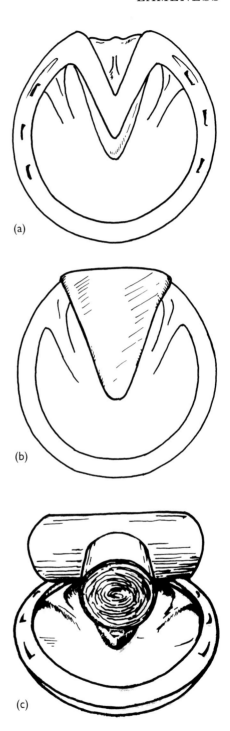

(a)

(b)

(c)

Fig. 49 Methods of supporting the frog, and thus the pedal bone, in the laminitic foot:
(a) The heart-bar shoe (fitted only after X-ray).
(b) The 'lily pad', a piece of moulded rubber placed over the frog and bandaged on.
(c) Rolls of bandage laid in a T-shape over the heels and frog, and then bandaged on.

125

Fig. 50 Representation of the corrective farriery needed to rebalance the laminitic foot:

(a) The position of the pedal bone within the normal foot.

(b) The rotated pedal bone in the laminitic foot.

(c) Lines representing the trimming necessary to rebalance the foot shown in (b).

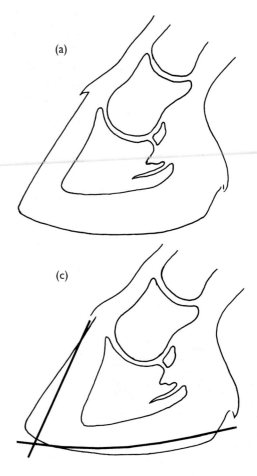

(a)

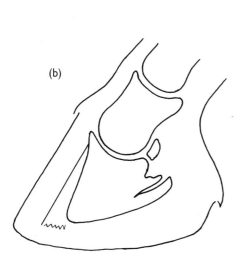

(b)

(c)

X-rays are useful, both to aid appropriate farriery, and also to give an accurate idea of the severity of the disease, and thus the likely outcome. Side views of the feet are taken, and the angle between the front wall of the hoof and the surface of the pedal bone is assessed. In the normal horse these are parallel (*see* Fig. 51). In the laminitic foot, rotation of the pedal bone causes it to deviate from the hoof wall (*see* Fig. 52), and the degree of deviation is a guide to prognosis.

If the pedal bone has rotated by less than 5 degrees, there is a fairly good prospect of recovery, but as the degree of rotation increases towards 15 degrees the chance of regaining full mobility becomes less and less. If there is more than 15 degrees of rotation, the prognosis is very poor. Similarly, if there is sinking of the pedal bone it is unlikely that the animal will be able to return to being an athlete.

If horses are not allowed to become overweight, laminitis may be avoided. The ribs are the best indicators of whether a horse is overweight: they should be easily detectable by feel, but not by eye. It is impossible to say how much food is appropriate for a particular horse, but high-energy and high-protein diets (for example, sugar

126

Fig. 51 X-ray of the normal foot.

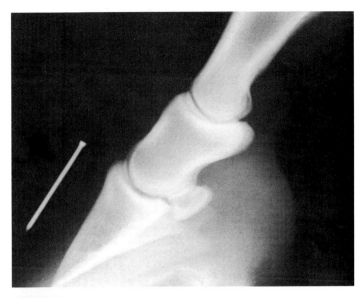

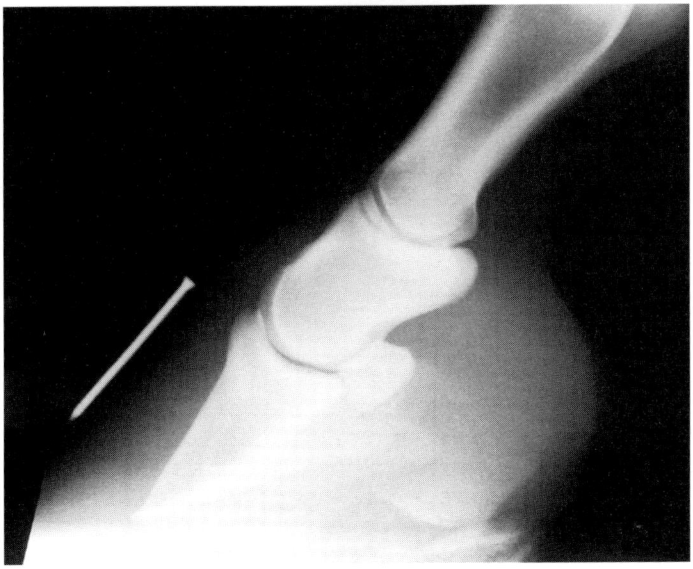

Fig. 52 X-ray of the laminitic foot.

beet, corn and other short feeds) should be avoided. Even when in work most ponies can derive enough energy from a forage diet (i.e. grass or hay with added hi-fi if necessary). Alfalfa hay is preferable to grass hay because it has less carbohydrate. Ponies on pasture can graze vast amounts of grass very quickly, so it is a good idea to limit them to a semi-bare paddock with perhaps an hour a day on grass during summer. Supplementing the diet with a biotin-rich formula may help to improve the quality of the hoof horn. Various herbal remedies claim to prevent laminitis and, whilst these may be useful, most are unproven.

Many horses and ponies have laminitis once in their lives and do go on to make full recoveries; but some, especially those that have a predisposition to the disease, are prone to repeat bouts. In such cases it is a good idea to make a habit of monitoring the pulse to the foot and the heat of the hoof daily, as well as keeping the horse fit and healthy with a regulated diet and exercise regime.

Sheared Heels

Severe imbalance of the foot can result in one heel being compressed more than the other so that the heels no longer make contact with the ground together. This unequal pressure eventually results in the heels' becoming separated from each other, hence the term sheared heels. On examination of the foot, the sulcus (groove) between the heels and along the frog can often be seen to be particularly deep (thrush is a common complicating factor); it may even be possible to move the heels independently of each other by hand. Contraction of the heels often follows.

Pain can be localized to the heel area using hoof-testers or nerve blocks. In the acute phase, treatment may involve the use of anti-inflammatory painkillers, but the most important thing is corrective farriery to rebalance the foot so that both heels strike the ground together and a shearing force no longer occurs between them. An egg-bar shoe is often used to provide bilateral support across the heels.

Navicular Syndrome

Navicular syndrome involves disease of the navicular bone and associated joints in the hoof, as well as the deep digital flexor tendon (DDFT) and the impar and suspensory ligaments. The navicular bone lies just behind and underneath the coffin joint (the joint between the pedal bone and the short pastern bone). It is slung at both ends by its suspensory ligaments and connected to the pedal bone by the impar ligament. The DDFT runs over it to insert itself on to the pedal bone (see Fig. 48).

Clinically, navicular syndrome causes chronic, progressive, usually bilateral, forelimb lameness. Foot pain may be localized to the heel area by the application of hoof-testers. Nerve blocks also aid diagnosis: anaesthesia of the palmar digital nerves just above the heel should alleviate the lameness, indicating that the pain originates from this area. In some cases, though, where the disease has progressed to involve the coffin joint as well, this joint may also need to be anaesthetized to alleviate lameness. Anaesthesia of the navicular bursa should alleviate pain.

Radiographs of the area should be studied, and these may show a number of changes in the navicular bone, although almost all the abnormalities that are seen in suspected navicular disease have also been seen in animals with no navicular disease, so diagnosis cannot be made on the strength of radiograph results alone. Radiographic changes include the development of thinner, and in some cases cystic, areas within the bone, as well as areas of increased density. In addition, bony changes on the edges of the bone may be seen extending into the soft- tissue structures, indicating instability.

There has been a great deal of discussion as to the likely cause of navicular syndrome, but none of the theories is proven. We know that if the conformation of a horse's feet falls outside a normal range, abnormal stresses occur, which are obviously magnified by higher exercise levels. These abnormal stresses may be particularly marked in the flexor tendons and the flexor surface of the navicular bone over which the tendons run. This is thought to stimulate adaptation within the bone to take account of increased stress, i.e., certain areas of the navicular bone thicken in order to help it bear the increased stress.

This thickening process gives rise to the most feasible theory of the cause of the syndrome, which is that in horses whose foot conformation falls outside even the normal range of abnormality – in other words, whose conformational abnormality is exceptional – or whose exercise level is excessive, the extent of the bone remodelling is exaggerated to the point that areas of the navicular bone are destroyed, and blood flow and blood pressure within the bone increases. All of this can create a vicious circle of bone destruction and reabsorption, leading to the pain and lameness that we identify as navicular syndrome.

From the description of the way navicular syndrome causes pain, it can be seen that treatment will rest, in part at least, on rebalancing of the foot. Corrective farriery is extremely important, and in most cases the toes is trimmed back more than the heel, or the heel is raised with wedges, to reduce strain through the DDFT and thus over the navicular bone. Egg-bar shoes are often used as they help to give support to the heels; wide-webbed shoes with rolled toes may also be helpful. Complete rest is rarely useful; instead, an exercise programme that involves an initial reduction in workload and then a gradual building up of exercise is needed. Anti-inflammatory medication is often administered, either orally, or via injection into the navicular bursa. Warfarin (an anti-coagulant) has been used to thin the blood and thus improve blood flow through the area, and some cases have responded dramatically to this treatment. However, the use of Warfarin requires regular monitoring of the blood's ability to clot: this is important in order to assess potential side-effects. Drugs that cause dilation of the blood vessels in the area, such as Isox-uprine hydrochloride and Trinitroglycerine gel, have also been used.

It has been proposed that cutting the suspensory ligaments of the navicular bone allows it to rebalance itself by relieving the tension through this ligament. Certainly this surgery has produced some good results, but since it has been found that most of the nerves supplying the navicular bone are associated with its suspensory ligaments, it is now thought that the cutting of these ligaments, and thus severing the nerves, merely removes the horse's ability to feel the pain rather than curing the condition.

Fractures

Fractures usually, but not always, cause lameness that is so severe that weight cannot be borne on the affected limb. Any lameness that is this severe requires prompt veterinary attention. In many cases, fractures in horses are untreatable because the huge stresses within equine bones make stabilization of breaks difficult, or even impossible. It can be difficult to justify the pain and stress (and the expense) involved in attempting to treat such injuries when the ultimate prognosis is not good.

Fractures may result either from abnormal stresses applied to a bone, or from direct trauma. Those caused by stress may or may not result in wounds; those caused by trauma are usually associated with skin wounds. The presence of open skin wounds worsens the prognosis because the likelihood of contamination and consequent infection is increased.

In severe cases, diagnosis of fractures is possible by clinical examination alone. (Where necessary, euthanasia may be carried out on the basis of such a clinical examination.) Most cases, however, require radiography for complete assessment. Where possible, this should be

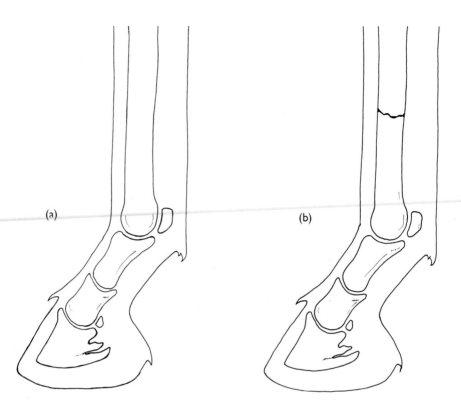

Fig. 53 Emergency veterinary attention and stabilization of a fracture: (a) represention of the normal cannon bone and pastern, and the necessary bandaging and padding (c) of the fractured leg shown in (b). In an emergency situation, a splint (d) is applied to support the fracture.

carried out *in situ* rather than moving the horse. If the horse does need to be taken to a hospital, a Robert Jones bandage and/or splint should be applied (*see* Fig. 53, and also Chapter 4) to protect the limb from further damage in transit. In addition, support bandages should be applied to the other limbs, as they will be carrying more weight than normal.

For less obvious fractures, such as minor stress or small chip fractures, nerve blocks and nuclear scintigraphy may be needed to localize the problem prior to radiography. In some cases (*see* box opposite) ultrasonography is also a useful diagnostic aid.

The emergency treatment of fractures consists of pain relief and temporary immobilization of the affected part, which helps to prevent further damage and provides more pain relief. Any further treatment may require referral to an equine hospital for surgery.

Treatment of fractures requires successful surgical stabilization of the site of the fracture and alignment of fragments to allow healing to occur. This is achieved, where possible, with screws, plates, wires or casts. Effective counteraction of the forces that are applied to the area is made particularly difficult in horses because of their sheer bulk and the extreme forces applied through their limbs. In addition, even when convalescent they tend to keep standing and so cannot be nursed as effectively as small animals and humans can.

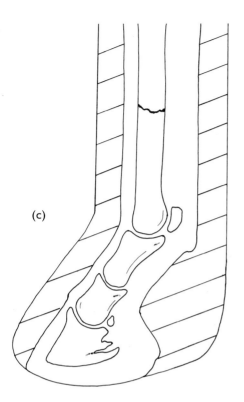

(c)

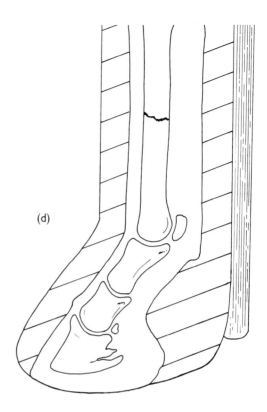

(d)

Fracture stabilization in the horse is therefore particularly difficult, hence the poor prognosis for recovery, and the consequent euthanasia of many horses with broken bones. In addition, the extra weight borne by the other limbs, particularly the contralateral (opposite) one, makes the horse susceptible to tendon strain (*see* pages 142–6) and laminitis (*see* pages 123–8) during the convalescent stages, which can be equally life-threatening.

Less serious cases may or may not require surgery, and sufficient rest may allow a return to athletic function, but horses that have sustained fractures rarely return to full work.

Stress Fractures
Stress fractures may involve the pedal bone and other phalangeal bones, the sesamoids, cannons and splint bones, as well as the small bones of the knee and hock. They occur as a result of abnormal strain in the area, and are seen most commonly in young racehorses.

Affected horses may show acute non-weight-bearing lameness or, particularly in the case of chip fractures, intermittent lameness. Surface fractures that involve only the cortex (outer surface) of the bone may cause mild lameness and may be seen radiographically as hairline fissure fractures and/or saucer fractures. The former usually run longitudinally up and down the bone, while the latter tend to occur on the dorsal surface of the cannon bone and may remain localized.

Radiography is required for diagnosis. Treatment may be based on box-rest and medication with anti-inflammatories, or surgery may be required to remove or stabilize fragments of bone. This may result in complete recovery, but, if the horse is exercised, catastrophic acute fractures can occur. Some of these fractures

131

can be stabilized with screws or plates, combined with casting of the limb; some are untreatable. The prognosis depends on the extent of the fracture, the number of fragments, and whether or not the joints are involved.

Fracture of the Pedal Bone

Fractures of the pedal bone are not always catastrophic. They are usually stress-related injuries that often occur following strenuous exercise on hard ground.

Although the horse with this type of fracture will be extremely lame, he may nevertheless be able to bear some weight on the limb because the encasing hoof acts almost like a splint, helping to keep the fracture stable. Typically, the horse avoids turning onto the affected foot and tends to point the foot when resting it. Clinical signs include heat in the foot and an increased digital pulse (see Chapter 2). In addition, hoof-testers applied across the sole elicit pain. Similar clinical signs are seen in horses with subsolar abscesses (see page 123), laminitis (see pages 123–8), and inflammatory disease of the pedal bone.

Radiographs are needed in order to assess the extent of the fracture (see Figs 54–55), and whether or not it involves the joint (those that do are much more painful, and may require surgery or may not be treatable). In most cases, treatment involves the application of a straight-bar or egg-bar shoe to provide maximal hoof stability, and box-rest for two to three months. Small breaks of the tip of the pedal bone may cause only mild pain and so may present as chronic lameness; in such cases, radiography and nerve blocks may be needed to confirm that a fracture is present.

Fracture of the Navicular Bone

Navicular bone fractures are extremely rare. They usually cause acute lameness localized to the foot, and are diagnosed radiographically. These fractures are very difficult to treat. Rest, and stabilization of the hoof with corrective shoeing, may result in healing. Surgical stabilization of the bone with screws has been attempted, but has rarely been successful. The prognosis is very poor.

Fracture of the Sesamoid Bones

Fracture of the sesamoid bones of the fetlock is often associated with suspensory ligament strain (see pages 142–6)), but it can occur independently.

Clinical signs, which are usually sufficient for diagnosis, are acute, severe lameness and, usually, obvious localized swelling that may be painful to the touch. Flexion of the fetlock also elicits pain. If both sesamoids are broken, there may be complete loss of support of the fetlock joint, which may then sink towards the ground. Radiography can determine the extent of the fractures. The surface of the sesamoid bones can also be seen using ultrasonography, and this may aid diagnosis.

Recovery is possible if treatment is prompt and appropriate, with surgical fixation of the fracture. However, if the suspensory ligaments are severely damaged, the prognosis may be extremely poor.

Fracture of the Splint Bone

Splint-bone fractures usually result from direct trauma. Swelling is seen on either the medial (inside) or lateral (outside) surface of the cannon bone, and the area is painful to the touch. In acute cases, the horse may be extremely lame at walk; in milder cases, lameness may be seen only at trot. Radiography is required for diagnosis and assessment of severity (see Fig. 56).

These injuries are less serious than fractures of weight-bearing bones, and rarely cause fatality. However, where there is also severe disruption of the adjacent suspensory ligament, the prognosis is less

Fig. 54 Side X-ray of a
fracture involving the
extensor process of the
pedal bone.

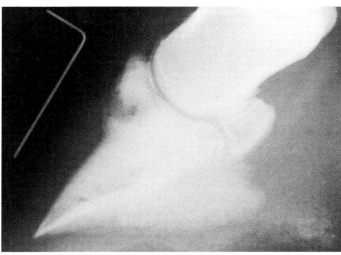

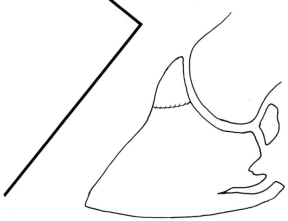

Fig. 55 Representation of the fracture
shown in the X-ray in Fig. 54.

favourable. If the skin is open, subsequent infection is a risk, and intensive antibiotic therapy will be necessary.

In many cases these fractures heal with adequate rest (often several months), but faster and more cosmetic results (i.e. less resulting bony swelling in the area) may be achieved with surgical fixation, or with removal of the fractured portion of the bone.

bone fractures, involve open wounds with fragments of broken bone visible within. Such cases are clearly disastrous. Radiography may be needed for full assessment. Treatable cases require internal fixation with screws and plates, combined with casting of the limb and several months of box-rest. Foals with these fractures have a better chance of survival than do adults.

Fracture of the Cannon Bone
Cannon-bone fractures that are caused by trauma may, like other transverse long-

Fracture of the Long Bone
Like those of the cannon bone, fractures of the higher long bones in the legs (i.e. the

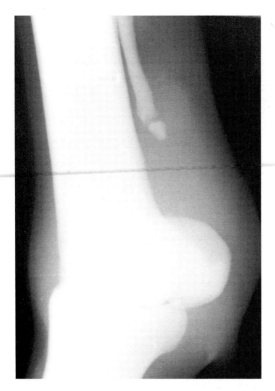

Fig. 56 X-ray of a fracture of the lower tip of a splint bone.

radius, ulna and humerus in the forelimb, and the tibia and femur in the hind limb – *see* Fig 47), on the whole carry very poor prognoses.

The horse is usually unable to bear weight on the affected limb, and since these fractures usually result from direct trauma, obvious swelling and concurrent skin wounds are common. In addition, by palpating the area you may be able to feel crepitus, or even hear it. Radiography is needed for complete assessment.

Those fractures that can be treated require surgical fixation with plates and months of box-rest; return to any kind of athletic function is unlikely, and treatment is usually reserved for those horses that have a future as breeding animals.

Fractures Involving Joints

Fractures involving joints are, in general, much more serious than those that do not: they tend to be more painful, more unstable, and damage to the cartilage in the area results in irregularity of the bone surface, predispoing it to inflammatory and arthritic changes. Whether or not a fracture involves a joint may be clinically apparent, but radiography is required for assessment.

Chip Fractures

With chip fractures of bones in the joints, small fragments of bone can cause varying degrees of lameness. There may be moderate, intermittent lameness as the fragment moves within the joint. Chip fractures most commonly occur in the fetlock, usually as a result of over-extending it while galloping. Nerve blocks and radiography usually permit diagnosis. Surgical removal of the fragment, combined with rest and anti-inflammatory medication, is often successful (although arthritis in later life can be expected).

Fractures of the small bones of the carpus (knee) and tarsus (hock) may take the form of small chip fractures or large slab fractures. These are usually stress related and are most commonly seen in young racehorses. Radiography is needed for diagnosis and assessment.

Carpal chip fractures usually cause only mild lameness that may be acutely associated with swelling in the front of the knee. Arthroscopic removal of these small fragments makes for the best prognosis. Depending on the size and position of the fragment, and whether or not there are already arthritic changes in the joint, the affected horse may in due course return to his original level of performance.

Slab fractures of the carpal or tarsal bones are much more serious than chip fractures, and result in severe (usually non-weight-bearing) lameness and swelling of the area. Flexion of the joint elicits further

---

Diagnosing pelvic fractures

Ultrasonographic examination of the rump area can allow diagnosis of a pelvic fracture to be made, in which case there may be no need to X-ray. This is just as well because radiography of the pelvic area in the horse usually requires general anaesthesia, and the positioning of the horse on his back (a manoeuvre necessitating the use of a winch and leg straps). Ultrasonographic examination or nuclear scintigraphy is therefore much preferred.

---

pain, and instability or crepitus may be felt. Some of these fractures can be stabilized with screws, but some are untreatable.

Fracture of the Scapula
Scapular fractures, which cause forelimb lameness with upper-limb pain, may be diagnosed on clinical examination, but require radiographic assessment. Treatment with long periods of box-rest can result in successful return to work.

Fracture of the Pelvis
Pelvic fractures usually cause bilateral hindlimb pain, lameness, and often a visible asymmetry of the pelvis (*see* Figs 30 and 57). Radiography may be needed for diagnosis, but ultrasonography is preferable (*see* box above). Most cases can be successfully treated with box-rest of several months; the exceptions are those in which the fracture involves nearby joints.

Fracture of the Spine
Though rare, spinal fractures usually result in such severe clinical signs (incoordination, collapse, paralysis) that euthanasia is carried out. The exception to this is sacral fracture (fracture of the lower spine at the level that it articulates with the pelvis, *see* Fig. 2), whose symptoms typically include bilateral hindlimb pain and lameness, tail weakness, and anal slackness caused by secondary nerve problems. In some cases abnormal sensation in the rump area occurs. It may be treated successfully with strict rest, but severe cases may necessitate euthanasia.

Joint-related Diseases

Long-term concussion is implicated in a variety of diseases that run a chronic course. Such problems include most types

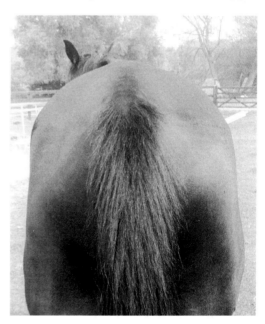

Fig. 57 This horse's pelvis is asymmetrical following a fracture. The right tuber coxa is lower than the left, while the tuber sacrale are even. The marked muscle wastage on the right indicates that the horse has been bearing the greater proportion of weight on the left.

135

of degenerative joint disease (DJD) and arthritis (in particular ringbone and bone spavin). Whilst these conditions are not caused by injury as such, they are associated with low-grade chronic wear and tear on joints, which results in loss of cartilage and bone breakdown combined with new bone formation. This initiates a vicious circle in which inflammation causes damage, which causes inflammation. The affected joints become swollen, and may be visibly so (see Fig. 58).

Arthritic disease most commonly affects high-motion joints because these are subjected to stresses to a greater degree than are low-motion ones. Other predisposing factors include the individual's conformation (joints that are offset and thus bear asymmetric strains are more susceptible to damage), bone maturity, exercising surface, and type of work. As the horse ages, most joints (especially the high-motion ones) will suffer some degree of cartilage damage and new bone formation in and around the weight-bearing surfaces. Heavy work and concussion speed this process, and the development of arthritis or degenerative joint disease is common in older working horses.

Ringbone

Ringbone is inflammation and new bone formation in and around the pastern and fetlock joints. Concussion is one of the main predisposing factors, but injuries such as wire wounds can also cause it. Many showjumpers develop ringbone in later life, perhaps as a result of the intense strains that pass through this area as a horse lands from a jump, when there is a tendency to overextend the fetlock and pastern joints.

Pasterns affected by ringbone typically have a bell-shaped appearance, and the new bone formation can easily be seen on X-rays (see Figs 59 and 60). If the joints are involved, lameness and stiffness often

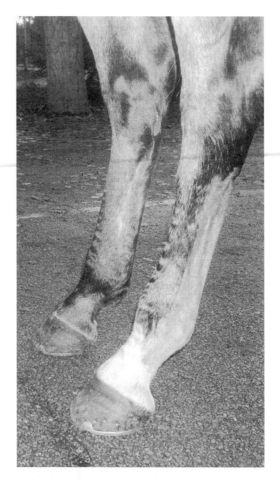

Fig. 58 Swelling of the fetlock joint and the area above it on this horse's left hind limb.

result. In some cases the new bone formation is localized around the edges of the joints, causing no problems, but in others it roughens the joint surfaces. Where mild lameness is apparent, the judicious use of anti-inflammatory painkillers combined with a programme of controlled exercise can help to maintain mobility. In severe cases, rest may be necessary and, in the worst cases, the disease progresses to the point at which the horse's quality of life is unacceptable.

Windgalls

These are swellings between the tendons just above the fetlock joints. Joints affected by arthritis may be visibly swollen, and in some cases windgalls are thought to be signs of arthritis. In fact, although windgalls do represent swelling of synovial structures associated with the fetlocks, they usually occur with no underlying disease, and no lameness. They are extremely common in older horses, and are rarely cause for concern. Attempts to treat them are rarely successful; they usually remain present despite rest, anti-inflammatory medication, or bandaging.

Sesamoiditis

Sesamoiditis is an inflammatory disease of the sesamoid bones. Although it results from concussion, poor conformation may be a predisposing factor. The suspensory ligament inserts onto the sesamoid bones, so inflammatory disease of the two is often connected, and associations with splints are also common. Lameness caused by sesamoiditis is localizable to the fetlock area with nerve blocks, but a pain response can often be elicited by direct palpation of the sesamoid bones, and in some cases swelling in this area can be seen. X-rays can confirm the presence of inflammatory

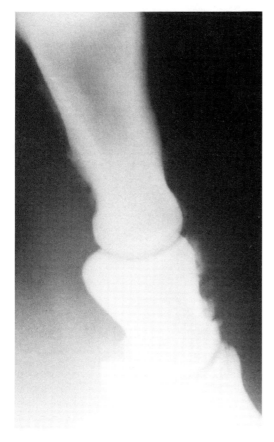

Fig. 59 X-ray showing arthritic change typical of ringbone.

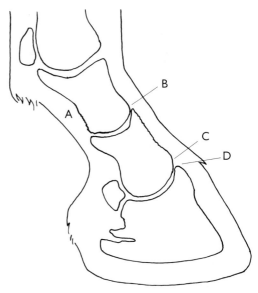

Fig. 60 Representation of the X-ray seen in Fig. 59 (a side view of the pastern and coffin joints), showing a severe case of ringbone involving arthritic change. There is roughening of the surface of the bone as a result of bone breakdown and new bone formation down the back of P1 (A) and down the front of P2 (B–C). In area (B) there is irregular bone impinging on the pastern joint, and in area (D) irregular bone impinges on the coffin joint and extends onto the pedal bone. This causes pain and joint stiffness.

changes involving the sesamoid bones. Rest and the use of anti-inflammatory medication may result in improvement of the condition, but it can take months or years before any progress is seen.

Splints

Splints form when inflammation occurs around the surface of the metacarpal (splint) bones and, in particular, in the area between the splint bones and the cannon bone. Localized pain and swelling results (see Fig. 61).

This condition is most often seen in young horses, and concussion (i.e. excessive work on hard ground) is often a predisposing factor, along with poor shoeing and foot balance. In some cases poor conformation is also a factor. An offset knee, for instance, transmits more weight down one side of the cannon bone than the other, and this makes the splint bone on this side (often the medial side) prone to inflammatory disease. The inflammation results in periostitis (bony swelling) at this site, which can be felt or seen.

Lameness is usually present only in the initial stages of the splint's development, and, if treated early, rest and the judicious use of anti-inflammatory medication and cold hosing usually results in a rapid recovery. The lump on the splint bone may then disappear completely, or it may merely be reduced. After the initial phase of rest, light work can be started again, but hard ground should be avoided for a time.

Splints are relatively common, but are rarely serious unless they are not treated promptly and large swellings are allowed to develop. If this happens, the knee joint, or the suspensory ligament which lies between the splint bones, can become involved, with potentially serious consequences. Large swelling of the splint bones can also increase the likelihood of their becoming further damaged by, for

instance, a brushing injury, and fractures of the splint bones are then more likely. Where complications do occur, X-rays of the area should be taken and, in some case, the suspensory ligament examined ultrasonographically. Sometimes surgery is needed to reduce large splints, or to remove fragments of fractured splints.

Bucked Shins and Dorsal Metacarpal Disease

Bucked shins are the result of concussion, causing a low-grade chronic inflammation of the front aspect of the cannon bone. The surface of the affected bone becomes inflamed, with consequent swelling, new bone formation, pain, and therefore lameness. Saucer and fissure fractures can also result (see page 132).

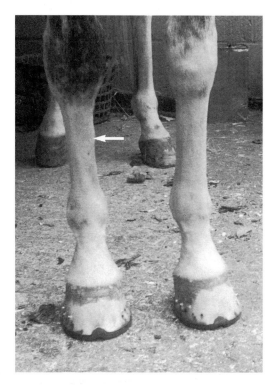

Fig. 61 This horse has small splints.

Rest and anti-inflammatory medication can make for complete recovery, but may give only temporary relief from lameness; in severe cases there may be little that can be done to ensure a complete recovery.

Similar symptoms can be seen as a result of bruising of the surface of the bone following kick injuries. The damaged periosteum (surface of the bone) becomes inflamed, usually causing localized swelling, significant pain and lameness, even if no fractures are present. Rest and anti-inflammatory medication usually ensure full recovery, although the surface of the bone may be left distorted (*see* Fig. 62)

Capped Joints
The capped joint can be mistaken for a swollen joint, but the true capped joint

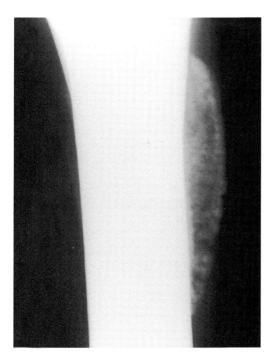

Fig. 62 X-ray showing proliferation on the surface of the cannon bone causing a hard lump following a kick injury in this area.

has an enlarged, fluid-filled sac (or acquired bursa) on the surface of the joint tip (such as the point of the elbow or hock). It is caused by repeated trauma to the area (of the sort that occurs when the horse continually lies down in the same position, bringing the hoof into contact with the joint).

If there are no complications, no lameness is apparent except in the acute phase. Although there is often a desire to remove the joint caps they are usually best left alone. Occasionally, however, infection necessitates drainage or removal.

In the acute phase the capped joint can be painful when touched. Without treatment, chronic enlargement of the area results (although this can also occur with treatment). Short-term treatment involves rest, cold-hosing/cold-packing and the use of anti-inflammatories. Surgical drainage of the fluid can improve matters, but can also make things worse if infection is introduced as a result. A pressure bandage can be useful. In heavy horses, sausage boots can be used to prevent the hoof traumatizing the elbows when lying down.

Bone Spavin
Like capped hocks and bog spavins, the bone spavin causes swelling of the hock, but the spavin is the result of degenerative joint disease (DJD). Hard work, particularly jumping, on hard ground, is a predisposing factor, and the condition is more common in horses with cow hocks (hocks that turn towards each other) or sickle hocks (in which the angle between hock and fetlock is too acute).

The spavin is characterized by bony irregularity, usually in the lower joints of the hock, and bony swelling and lameness that is localizable to the area. If the hock is X-rayed (*see* Figs 63–65), areas of bone lysis (disintegration) and new bone formation are seen, and the joint spaces are lost. In most cases the disease is self-limiting: if the horse continues light work (and he may need painkilling medication to allow him to do this), the affected joints eventually fuse and stop being uncomfortable. Since the joints affected are commonly the low-motion joints, the horse is usually able to work again once bone fusion has taken place. Occasionally, however, fusion does not occur spontaneously, and has to be achieved surgically.

Bog Spavin

Bog spavin also causes hock swelling, but in this case the swelling is soft because it is characterized by the production of excess joint fluid. The cause is often unidentifiable, but poor conformation is thought to be a predisposing factor. It is not usually associated with lameness, so treatment is not usually necessary.

Curb

Curbs are swellings on the back of the hock. They cause this part of the joint to lose its clean, straight appearance and become curved. A true curb is caused by strain of the plantar ligament (the ligament that holds the back of the hock in line), and can result in weakness and pain in this area. While curbs are usually the result of direct trauma or a fall, horses that are sickle hocked are particularly prone to developing them.

In the acute stage of the disease – when swelling, heat and pain, and mild lameness are apparent – rest, topical treatment (in the form of cold packs or cooling lotions), and the use of non-steroidal anti-inflammatory drugs are indicated; most cases will resolve themselves within two to four weeks. In chronic cases some swelling will remain, but there is usually no lameness.

True curbs can be differentiated from other problems ultrasonographically. In young horses (usually yearlings), they are commonly associated with damage or collapse of some of the hock bones, so affected horses that are within this age group should be X-rayed.

Thoroughpin

This condition is often confused with curbs. It consists of distension of the tarsal sheath which surrounds the hock, and is seen as a soft, fluid-filled swelling on either side of the hock, just above the point of the hock. Most cases are seen in young horses for no apparent reason, and with no signs of lameness. In the acute phase, cold-hosing or cold-packing, and anti-inflammatory medication may be helpful, but many cases are unresponsive to treatment.

Upward Fixation of the Patella

This condition causes the patella or knee cap to remain locked as the horse starts to move off. In consequence he cannot bend his knee, and it therefore becomes stretched out behind him. The patella can usually be 'unlocked' either by backing the horse up, or by straightening the leg out behind him. In most cases, no clinical treatment is needed, although surgical treatment can prevent it from happening.

The condition is not uncommon in young horses, and appears to be hereditary in some pony breeds. However, it is most often related to development, and it usually ceases when the horse becomes fit. Increasing the muscle tone of the thigh and rump can therefore prevent it.

Dislocation of the Hip

This extremely rare condition follows trauma. It usually renders the horse unable to bear weight on the affected limb, and manipulation of the limb is resented.

140

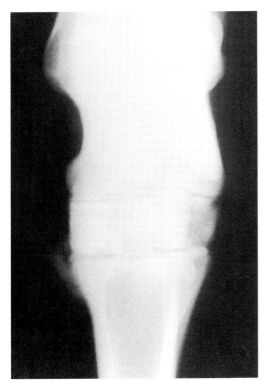

Fig. 63 X-ray showing bone spavin in the left hock.

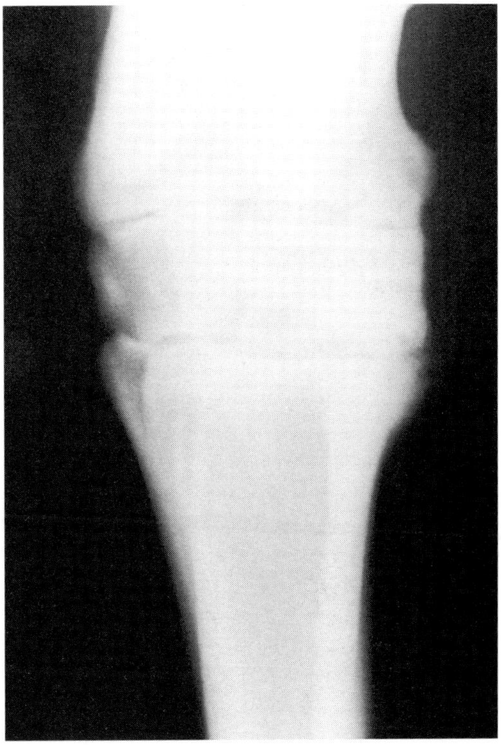

Fig. 64 X-ray showing bone spavin in the right hock of the same horse.

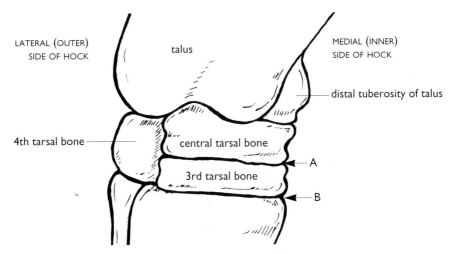

LATERAL (OUTER)
SIDE OF HOCK

talus

MEDIAL (INNER)
SIDE OF HOCK

distal tuberosity of talus

4th tarsal bone

central tarsal bone

3rd tarsal bone

A

B

Fig. 65 Representation of the common sites of disease (A and B) in cases of bone spavin in a front-to-back view of the hock.

Without X-rays, it is difficult to distinguish a dislocated hip from fracture of the femur or pelvis. Attempts to replace the hip in its joint under anaesthesia are rarely successful, and euthanasia is often necessary.

Joint Infections
Infection of a joint (or septic arthritis/synovitis) can follow infection of a wound in the vicinity of a joint (*see* Chapter 8) or can occur when bacteria are carried to a joint in the bloodstream. The result is usually a very painful, swollen, hot joint causing lameness so severe that the horse is unable to bear weight on the affected limb. The horse becomes ill, and often has a high temperature. Treatment with antibiotics alone is rarely effective; along with intensive antibiotic therapy, flushing

of the joint with large volumes of fluid may be necessary. This requires surgery, and may have to be done under general anaesthesia. Some horses do not respond to treatment and have to be euthanased.

Tendon Injuries

Tendon injuries are stress-related. They may accompany wounds in the back part of the lower limbs, but can occur with no associated skin deficits. The latter type often appears at first to be innocuous, but both types have the potential to cause disease so severe that the horse may not fully recover. This is of particular relevance to performance horses, which may never be able to compete at the same standard again.

Anatomy of the flexor tendons

The flexor tendons run down the back of each limb to the feet. They provide support to the back of the limbs during the weight-bearing phase of the stride, and control movement of the lower limb through much of its range. They are also involved in the stay apparatus, which allows the horse to stand, even when the muscles are relaxed, whilst sleeping. The extensor tendons, which run down the front of each limb, are also important in maintaining the integrity of the limbs, but since their primary involvement in movement is during the off-ground phase of the stride, they have much less force to bear. Lameness resulting from extensor tendon injury is extremely uncommon. The flexor tendons, however, are much more liable to injury, and to consequent severe lameness.

The flexor tendons consist of the superficial digital flexor tendon (SDFT), the deep digital flexor tendon (DDFT), the check ligament (CL), and the suspensory ligament (SL). (*See* Fig. 46.) The SDFT originates from the superficial digital muscle above the knee or hock, and runs down the back of the limb, under the skin, and outside the DDFT. The DDFT also originates

from its muscle above the knee or hock, and it runs down to be joined by the check ligament in the mid-cannon area. The combined tendon continues under the SDFT to below the fetlock, at which level the SDFT splits, and wraps itself round the DDFT on either side to insert into the phalangeal bones on either side of the pastern joint. The DDFT continues down, passing over the navicular bone, and attaches to the pedal bone. The SL originates from the back of the knee or hock, runs down the back of the cannon bone, almost between the splint bones, and splits into two above the fetlock where it is attached to the two sesamoid bones.

Each of these structures consist of parallel elastic fibres contained in a sheath-like coating. They form strap-like structures that are oval in cross-section, and average approximately ⅜in (1cm) across. They bear tremendous forces through a very small area, which is one of the reasons why they can easily become damaged. In addition, the majority of the blood supply comes from the ends of the tendons, so the mid-sections tend to have less blood supply and are therefore more susceptible to injury.

The early recognition of tendon injuries is of paramount importance in finding the appropriate treatment and so providing a horse with the best chance of recovery.

Tendon Strains
When normal tendons are palpated, it is often possible to distinguish the superficial digital flexor tendon (SDFT) from the deep digital flexor tendon (DDFT), particularly if the leg is lifted, and the tension on the tendons is thus released. Palpation of the check ligament (CL) and suspensory ligament (SL) is not really possible, except at the level where the SL branches to the sides and up towards the skin surface to the sesamoid bones. Even if you cannot feel this much detail, it is a good idea to get into the habit of feeling your horse's legs regularly. Run your hands down the back of each leg, from the knee or hock to the fetlock and beyond. Once you are used to the way they feel, any warmth or swelling in the area will become easily recognizable to you, and it will only take only a few seconds to check each leg every time you come back from a ride or bring your horse in from the field.

A strained tendon is the result of excessive stress passing through it. Damage takes the form of swelling (caused by inflammation within the tendon sheath) and fibre rupture. Rupture of the fibres may cause further swelling of the tendon as inflammatory chemicals are released, and, if large numbers of adjacent fibres rupture, cavities (core lesions) between the remaining fibres can form within the tendons. The build-up of inflammatory fluid between tendon fibres and within core lesions exerts pressure on the remaining fibres, damaging them and exacerbating the problem. It is important, therefore, to recognize tendon injuries promptly, so that measures to reduce ongoing inflammation can be taken.

Slight tendon strains, involving some swelling within the tendons and rupture of only a few fibres, tend to present with symptoms as vague as slight warmth and swelling; the horse may not even be lame. With more severe strains, involving rupture of more fibres, and greater swelling, there may be obvious signs of lameness, and the tendons will probably feel enlarged. In addition, inflammation causes swelling under the skin and around the tendons so that the borders of the tendons may no longer be felt. Attempts to feel and squeeze the tendons often cause pain, as does deep palpation between the splint bones if the SL is involved.

Tendon Lacerations and Penetrations
Tendon lacerations can be associated with wounds on the back of the lower limbs. When any wounds occur in this area, the possibility of tendon involvement should be considered, and veterinary treatment should be sought within four to eight hours (*see* Chapter 8). Penetration of the tendon sheath can occur with few clinical signs other than the presence of a wound (*see* Fig. 37), and can, without appropriate treatment, lead to irreversible infection of the tendon sheath, which can prove fatal. Deeper cuts involving a significant part of the tendons themselves cause more immediate clinical signs: depending on the extent of tendon damage, there may be varying degrees of backward collapse of the fetlock towards the ground. Damage to deeper structures, including the SL, which results in total disruption of the flexor structures, causes the fetlock to drop with concurrent lifting of the toe.

If you notice slight heat or swelling in the area, even without lameness, a tendon strain should be suspected. It is a good idea to institute box-rest, and to apply cold-hosing or cold boots to the area (ice is best avoided because it can actually cause burning). It is also a good idea to apply support bandages, not only to the affected limb, but also to the one on the other side.

143

Support, avoidance of exercise, and cooling will help to reduce further inflammation and damage. If within a day or so the legs feel completely normal, then turnout, or very light exercise can be tried, and the tendons reassessed afterwards.

If you suspect a more serious injury (there are signs of lameness, and/or excessive heat or obvious swelling), you should call the vet within 24 hours as well as instituting box-rest and hosing. This is important, because the vet is best placed to assess the injury and determine an appropriate regime of rest and/or controlled exercise.

If wounds are present, cold-hosing should be avoided as it can force bacteria into the wounds. Instead, the wound should be gently cleaned with dilute antiseptic (see Chapter 4) and urgent veterinary attention sought. An exact diagnosis must be made promptly because delaying treatment can endanger the horse's life. Treatment at an equine hospital may be necessary.

Where a tendon strain is suspected, ultrasound scanning is advisable for precise diagnosis. Scanning is often delayed,

however, until about a week after the injury, when ongoing inflammation has been brought under control with anti-inflammatory drugs such as phenylbutazone (bute). Complete assessment of the severity of the strain should then be possible. When both the structures involved,

Ultrasonographic examination of the tendons

Ultrasonography allows images of the tendons in both cross-section and long-section to be seen on screen. In cross-section, the tendon fibres look like white dots, and in long section like white lines, so that in cross-sectional views the tendon takes on a stippled appearance. Where fibre rupture or laceration occurs, the tendon-fibre pattern is lost, and black areas are seen on the screen. These represent accumulations of inflammatory fluid. In addition, swelling causes increases in cross-sectional areas of the tendon, which can be quantified, and the area occupied by the lesion can be assessed.

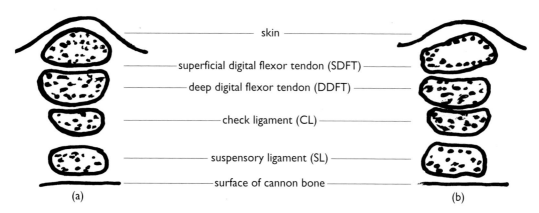

Fig. 66 Cross-sectional representation of a normal and abnormal ultrasound scan in the upper cannon area. (a) The normal tendon, apparent from the regular fibre consistency indicated by the black dots. (b) A limb with a severe core lesion of the superficial digital flexor tendon (SDFT), seen as a white area, which indicates lack of fibre consistency. (Note that in an original scan, the black and white areas shown in this illustration would appear in reverse.)

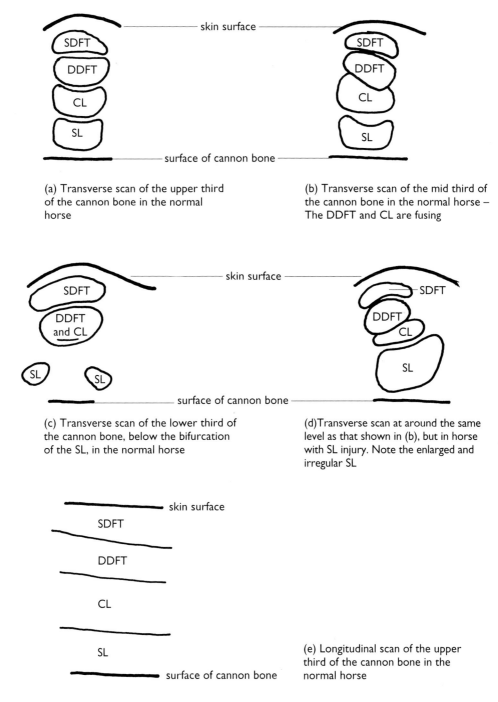

Fig. 67 *Representation of some normal and abnormal ultrasound scans of the flexor tendons.*

and the severity of the damage, are assessed, the necessary period of box-rest may be determined. Serial scanning to monitor healing enables the vet to judge when the tendon is strong enough to begin a controlled exercise regime, and when the levels of exercise can be safely increased. This keeps the loading of the tendon to within its capabilities during the healing phase of a tendon injury, and thus minimizes the chance of re-injury.

Tendon injuries: the prognosis

The prognosis of a tendon injury depends on a combination of the structures involved, the degree of fibre damage, and the ability of the horse to rest and to heal. Constructing an entire treatment plan based on a single scan is rarely possible; instead, treatment and appropriate controlled exercise regimes are worked out in stages, with the horse being serially scanned (often every four to eight weeks or so) to allow continual monitoring of the case, and to allow the timing of further exercise to be planned according to the state of healing.

On the whole, superficial digital flexor tendon injuries are less serious than those involving the deep digital flexor tendon. Suspensory ligament injuries can be very serious, particularly If the point of their insertion on the sesamoids is involved. Diffuse injuries tend to be less serious than those in which there is a large core lesion. Those injuries that include the tendon sheath have the potential to precipitate the formation of adhesions between the different tendon structures during healing, and this can cause ongoing complications.

With any tendon damage that occurs, the body institutes replacement with fibrous tissue during healing, and so the area will always be more prone to injuries in the future, both in the area of the scar tissue and in the area of the junction between this and the healthy tissue. Prompt, appropriate treatment of tendon injuries, however, minimizes the risk of future complications.

Superficial Digital Flexor Tendon Luxation

Superficial digital flexor tendon (SDFT) luxation can cause an odd swelling in the area of the hock. The SDFT normally travels over the very point of the hock (see Fig. 46). Occasionally, trauma or twisting of the leg can tear the connections of the SDFT and cause it to slip sideways off the point of the hock and come to lie on the outside of the hock. In the acute phase these horses are lame and may be distressed.

Box-rest, cold-hosing or cold-packing, and anti-inflammatory painkillers are advisable. In many cases, resumption of light work is possible after the acute phase of the disease as the tendon can continue to perform its function in its new position. However, the gait of the horse will look slightly odd. Surgery to replace the tendon in the correct position on the point of the hock has been carried out but is rarely successful.

Ligament Injuries

Ligaments join bones together and create stability in the joints.

In some cases, ligament strain will result in arthritic change at the junction between the ligaments and the bone. For instance, poor foot balance combined with excessive concussion can cause excessive strains in the joints, and consequently ligament damage, which can in turn result in arthritic change (see Fig. 68).

Muscle Rupture

Muscle rupture is a relatively uncommon cause of lameness in the horse, but it can occur following trauma, falls, or sliding. In most cases, local swelling is evident, and box-rest and anti-inflammatory treatment are necessary in the acute phase. The affected muscle often heals

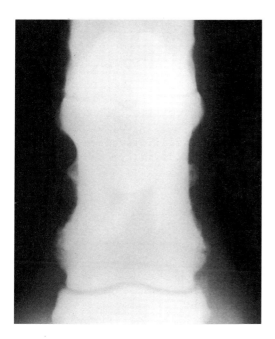

Fig. 68 X-ray showing inflammatory bone change in the first phalanx (long pastern bone).

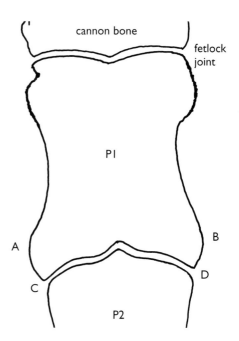

Fig. 69 Representation of the abnormalities shown in the X-ray in Fig. 68 (a front-to-back view of the fetlock and pastern joints). Bone breakdown and new bone formation have caused bone irregularity and roughening in areas A and B. These areas correspond to the origins of the collateral ligaments, which give support to the pastern, so the bone condition may relate to disease of these ligaments. There is also arthritic change in the pastern joint, seen as irregularity in areas C and D. These changes, which produced joint pain and stiffness, were thought to be the result of poor foot balance causing excessive side-to-side movements in the pastern joint.

alone, although fibrosis and subsequent stiffness of the area can result. Physiotherapy treatment can be helpful.

Peroneus Tertius Rupture

One particular type of muscle rupture that is not uncommon in the horse is rupture of the peroneus tertius muscle. This tiny muscle runs from above the stifle to below the hock, and is an important part of the reciprocal apparatus that ensures that a horse cannot normally flex or extend his hock and stifle independently. If the peroneus tertius becomes ruptured the stifle can be flexed whilst the hock is extended (*see* Fig. 70). Affected horses are lame initially, but can bear weight on the limb, although often the affected leg will tremble as it is put to the ground. Box-rest and anti-inflammatories are needed to

encourage healing of this muscle, and a support bandage may be necessary. Some cases will make a complete recovery.

Nerve Damage

Nerve-related injuries are comparatively rare in the horse. When they do occur, they are usually the result of direct trauma. In

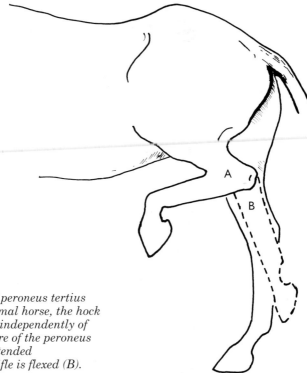

Fig. 70 Representation of peroneus tertius muscle rupture. In the normal horse, the hock and stifle cannot be flexed independently of each other (A). After rupture of the peroneus muscle, the hock can be extended (straightened) when the stifle is flexed (B).

many cases they are seen concurrently with either fractures or wounds that involve arterial bleeding, since many of the nerves lie adjacent to arteries.

The significance of these injuries depends on the degree of damage sustained by the affected nerve. In cases where concussion of the nerve occurs, spontaneous recovery may occur over several weeks, and this process can be aided with anti-inflammatory medication. In cases where transection of a nerve occurs, it may not recover, and consequent muscle wastage can progress to the point that mechanical changes to the gait result. Nerve damage can also cause the loss of sensation in a particular area. Wounds in the area below the back of the fetlock, for instance, can involve the nerves to the foot, and can therefore result in loss of sensation in the foot.

Radial-Nerve Paralysis
Radial-nerve paralysis can occur concurrently with fractures or wounds in the elbow area. This results in a dropped appearance of the elbow and lameness.

Sweeney
This is paralysis of the supra-scapular nerve, which courses round the front of the shoulder blade. The condition occurs as a result of direct damage to the nerve (most often caused by the shafts in driving injuries). The consequent loss of nerve supply to the shoulder muscles causes them to waste away, thereby increasing the prominence of the ridge of the shoulder blade. Low-grade mechanical lameness results, sometimes characterized by the shoulder's appearing to pop outwards as the horse bears weight on the affected limb.

Conclusion

Every horse is an individual, and I would encourage all horse owners to become as familiar as possible with their own horses, which means observing them on a day-to-day basis. Learn how your horse's legs feel, what his normal pulse rate is, and his normal temperature; know his moods and his normal behaviour. This will help you to recognize subtle signs of problems at the earliest possible stage, and thus give him the best chance of a full recovery from any disease or ailment. Having said this, keeping your horse healthy is not only a matter of noticing signs of disease early, and treating problems in a prompt and appropriate manner. Of the utmost importance is managing him in an environment that is safe.

I hope this book will help you to choose the best course of action in any particular situation, and that it will help to explain the possible consequences of various problems. However, every situation is different, and I cannot overemphasize the importance of discussing your horse's individual needs with your own vet, and following his advice.

Fig. 71 The author and her horse.

Appendix: Medication

ANTIBIOTICS

A limited number of different types of antibiotic are available for use in horses. The different types are prescribed in different applications, depending on the condition to be treated. For instance, mild skin, wound or chest infections may respond well to oral antibiotics, whilst infections in joint wounds may require the types that need to be injected either into a muscle or into a vein. Other infections, such as those of the eyes, may require a local or topical application.

ANTI-INFLAMMATORIES

The main anti-inflammatory agent used in equine medicine is phenylbutazone ('bute'), which is used to treat lameness, as well as other inflammation-related conditions, such as skin irritation. Other oral anti-inflammatories are licensed for use in equines, but on the whole they are more expensive and potential side-effects make them unsuitable for long-term use.

Some types of lameness may be treated by applying drugs that reduce joint inflammation and cartilage damage directly into the affected joints, or by intramuscular or intravenous injection.

Some types of inflammation that do not respond particularly well to the non-steroidal group of anti-inflammatories –

such as some skin or respiratory problems – can be treated using steroid medication, but this should be used with care as there are potential side-effects. These include depression of the immune system, and inhibition of healing, as well as increasing the likelihood of laminitis developing.

Topical anti-inflammatories, which include a variety of poultices and liniments such as DMSO and Tensolvet, can also be helpful in some cases.

WORMERS

Available wormers can be divided into three groups of drugs: the benzimidazoles

Phenylbutazone legislation

At the time of writing, European legislation classifies the horse as a food-producing animal, and phenylbutazone is not licensed for use in food-producing animals. However, rather than ban the use of bute in horses outright, UK legislation allows it to be prescribed as long as the horse never enters the human food chain. This is why the owner of any horse prescribed bute must sign a certificate guaranteeing that the horse will never enter the human food chain; if at any time the horse is sold on, this certificate must be passed to the new owner.

(such as Panacur, Telmin), the ivermectins (such as Eqvalan, Furexel, Panomec Equest) and the pyrantels (such as Pyratape P, Strongid P) are all licensed for oral use only in the horse, and, depending on each brand's formulations, can be given as powder or granules in food, or directly into the mouth in a paste form.

No wormer treats all the different types of worms, and different types of wormers need to be used at different times of year to effectively avoid worm infestation (*see* Chapter 1 for more details).

All medication has a use-by date. It is important to check this and to make sure that the drug you are going to give your horse has not expired. When you obtain the drug, also check any instructions on the packaging regarding its storage, and ensure that you follow such instructions as it may otherwise lose its efficacy. (Ask your vet for advice if necessary.) It is always important, whatever drug is being used, that the full dose is given for the prescribed number of days.

HOW TO GIVE MEDICATION

Oral

To encourage your horse to take an oral medicine, you can try feeding the powder or granules in food that the horse normally likes. Molassed food hides flavours better than unmolassed food does. The addition of titbits, such as apples, carrots, and so on, can increase palatability of 'doctored' food. And for horses that like mints, peppermint oil can be added. Alternatively, drugs may be hidden within an apple or carrot by coring out a portion, introducing the medicine, and plugging the hole through which you introduced it. Drugs that come in the form of small tablets can be given wedged within a polo mint. Some drugs are now available with palatable flavourings such as peppermint or cocoa, and they can be very helpful.

Horses that will not take drugs in feed may have to be forced to take it directly by mouth. Many drugs are available in a paste form; those that aren't can, in most cases (check first with your vet), be mixed with water to form a paste that can then be administered by oral syringe.

When giving drugs by syringe in a paste form it is a good idea to have a helper holding the horse's head down. Nose-twitching the horse (*see* page 40) may also be helpful in order to aid control of the head and to help the horse to relax. The horse's head should be carefully steadied, and the tip of the syringe should be inserted at the side of the mouth, pointing up towards the back of the tongue. The medication should be introduced directly onto the tongue. Holding the horse's head up, and trying to keep his mouth shut may prevent him spitting it straight out!

Injection

Where horses will not take oral medication, or where intramuscular or intravenous medication is more appropriate, regular injections may be needed. Intramuscular injections may be given by the horse owner under veterinary guidance or supervision, but intravenous injections should only ever be given by vets. If your vet wishes you to give your horse a course of intramuscular injections, do ask him to show you how to do it. Whilst an outline of the procedure is given below, a written description of the technique is no substitute for being shown the appropriate sites and method on a horse.

Giving Intramuscular injections
The bottle of medication should first be shaken thoroughly to ensure that it is well mixed. In some cases, as with Penicillin, this may be difficult; then it is a good idea

to store the medication at room temperature rather than allowing it to get cold as this will aid mixing and withdrawal of the dose. In any case, allowing a drug to reach room temperature before giving it makes it less uncomfortable for the horse.

After shaking the bottle, swab the rubber entry point with cotton wool soaked in surgical spirit to remove any bacteria. Up-end the bottle and insert the needle connected to the syringe. Be sure not to allow the needle to make contact with any other object; if it does so discard it and use a clean one. Withdraw the correct dose of medication into the syringe. If you find some air has entered the syringe, allow it to rise towards the needle and then express it to ensure you have the correct dose of the drug within the syringe. If you find it difficult to withdraw the drug from the bottle, try injecting air into the bottle first, as this will ease the process. (This should not be done unless it is absolutely necessary as it may allow the entry of bacteria into the bottle.)

Once you have the correct volume of medication within the syringe, remove the needle and insert it into the horse as described below.

There are several sites on the horse that can be used for intramuscular injections,

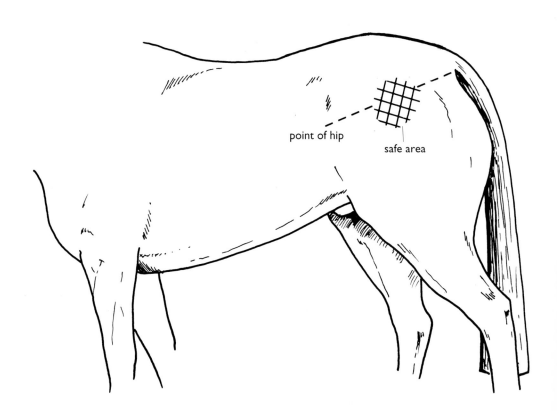

point of hip

safe area

Fig. 72 The safe area in which to administer an intramuscular injection in the rump is halfway between the point of the hips and the tail bone.

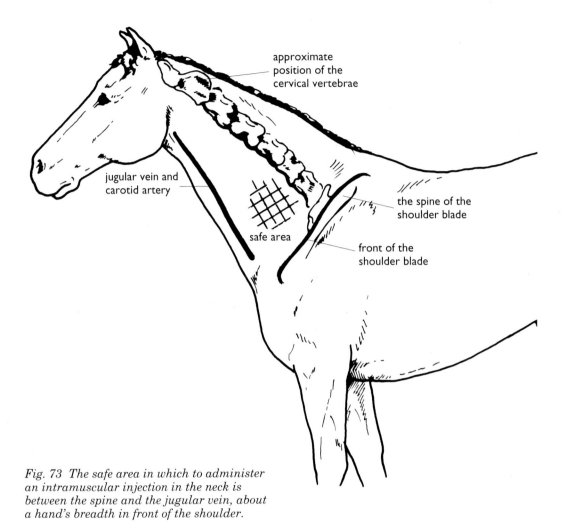

Fig. 73 The safe area in which to administer an intramuscular injection in the neck is between the spine and the jugular vein, about a hand's breadth in front of the shoulder.

but in most cases the easiest to use is the rump, since there is a large volume of muscle here, and few other structures that can be damaged. In adult horses the neck may also be used safely for injections if instructions are followed carefully.

The rump site (*see* Fig. 72) is approximately halfway along an imaginary line between the point of the hip and the tail base. In this area the needle can be safely and confidently introduced.

In the neck (*see* Fig. 73), a needle can be introduced about a hand's breadth back from the front of the shoulder, halfway between the underside of the neck and the upper side of the neck.

In either case the horse should be held or restrained by a handler, rather than tied up. The site to be injected should be swabbed with cotton wool soaked in surgical spirit. The site should be thumped once or twice and the needle then introduced

153

quickly and firmly, perpendicular to the skin, right up to the hub. The syringe should then be attached firmly to the needle and the plunger withdrawn slightly. **If there is any sign of blood entering the hub, the drug should not be injected**. If blood is seen, the needle should be removed, and replaced in a slightly different place, and the process repeated. If no blood is seen, the plunger of the syringe can be depressed, and the injection given. After the needle has been removed, the area can be rubbed to relieve any discomfort.

Complications include fractiousness on the part of the horse – do remember that horses can and will kick, so keep as far forward as possible when giving an injection into the rump. It is important to prevent human injury, so if you cannot safely inject your horse then contact your vet who may be able to arrange alternative medication or may arrange daily visits to give necessary injections.

Horses often are uncomfortable at the site of the injection for 24 to 48 hours, and so repeat injections should be given at another site, or the site should be rotated on a daily basis. If swelling is seen at the site of a neck injection, food and water may need to be provided from a raised level. Swelling at any site can also cause temporary lameness in the nearest limb. If swelling occurs, your vet should be contacted, as treatment with anti-inflammatory drugs may be needed, or a change in medication may be appropriate. Occasionally such a swelling develops into an abscess despite the most careful of injection techniques, and this may also require veterinary attention. Other complications include allergy to the drug used, which can result in symptoms ranging from pain and swelling at the injection site to sweating, colic and collapse. The latter signs necessitate veterinary attention and cessation of treatment with the drug that caused them.

Drugs for the Eye

Application of drugs to the surface of the eye, such as ointments or drops, should **only** be done where prescribed by a veterinary surgeon. The exception to this is the use of plain, cooled, boiled water applied with clean cotton wool to clean eyes where necessary. Use of inappropriate medication can cause damage to the eye.

In most cases application of drugs to the eye necessitates the presence of a helper to hold and restrain the horse. The head should be steadied. Using the finger and thumb of the left hand the lids can be parted, and the ointment can be applied using the right hand either directly onto the surface of the eye or onto the inside of the lower eyelid (*see* Fig. 74). Touching the tip of the nozzle onto the eye or eyelids should be avoided as this can result in bacteria being transferred onto the end of the tube and reintroduced later. Instead the ointment or drops should be allowed to drop into place on the surface of the eye from a slight distance. As the horse blinks, the drug will then be spread across the surface of the eye and its associated membranes.

Drugs for the Skin

A variety of drugs are available for use on the skin. When using medication, the instructions should be followed carefully. There are few preparations that should be used on open wounds or damaged skin, since many lotions can cause further damage. It is best to stick to cleaning such areas with plain boiled water to which either salt (1 teaspoon to 1 pint) has been added or dilute iodine or chlorhexidine solution. These solutions can be made by mixing a 0.1 per cent solution of povidone iodine (1 measure of Pevidine scrub in 7.5 measures water) or a 0.05 per cent solution of chlorhexidine (1 measure of Hibiscrub in 40 measures of water).

Fig. 74 Applying medication to the eye.

After this, drugs such as Intrasite can be applied to the damaged tissue to encourage granulation, caustic powders can be applied carefully under veterinary guidance to prevent the development of proud flesh, and wound powders/dressings may be applied with care to shallow wounds.

Drugs containing cortico-steroids can be used topically to reduce inflammation in the skin, but since these can also delay or suppress healing they are rarely appropriate for use on damaged skin. The use of these and other drugs should be carried out only after discussion with your vet.

In some cases the use of cold, heat and pressure can be quite as dangerous as the use of inappropriate topical medication. Intense heat or ice can damage the blood supply to skin and can result in necrosis of the skin and subsequent sloughing. Similar signs can be seen on removing pressure bandages that have been applied too tightly and left on too long. Heat or cold should be applied in the form of a pack, or from a hose for periods of 20 minutes or so at a time, up to three or four times daily. Ice-packs are best avoided, because cold water reduces inflammation just as effectively as ice does and is less likely to cause damage. Pressure bandages, where used, should be applied over-sufficient padding, and should changed at least twice daily (*see* Chapter 4).

Glossary

anaesthesia the rendering of part (local), or all (general) of the body insensitive to pain.

aneurysm the dilation of a blood vessel following a weakening in its walls, and resulting in a pulsating sac of blood that can rupture, which can lead to sudden and severe loss of blood.

antibacterial having activity against bacteria, such as killing them or preventing their reproduction.

antibiotic *see* antibacterial.

antihelminthic having activity against helminth-type parasites (worms).

anti-inflammatory of substances that act against inflammation.

antiparasitic having activity against parasites (worms, mites, or lice, etc.).

antiseptic having activity against infection.

arthritis inflammatory disease of a joint.

ataxia loss of strength of movement; weakness.

bilateral of both sides (cf. unilateral, contralateral).

bursa a fluid-filled sac, often found overlying and protecting a joint or bony prominence.

caudal of the side nearest the back end of the horse (cf. cranial).

closed fracture a fracture that is not associated with a skin wound (cf. open fracture).

colic abdominal pain.

coma profound unconsciousness.

concussion temporary loss of consciousness following an injury, such as a blow to the head.

contralateral of the opposite side (cf. bilateral, unilateral).

corpora nigra normal cyst-like swellings attached to the upper margin of the iris in the eye.

cortex outer layers of tissue in bone and many types of organ (cf. medulla).

cranial of the side nearest the front end of the horse (cf. caudal).

crepitus the crunchy sound and sensation caused by movement of damaged (e.g. broken or arthritic) bone.

de-gloving injury wound that removes all or most of the skin from an area of a limb.

desmitis inflammatory disease of a ligament.

diaphragm muscular boundary between the chest and abdomen.

diastole the pause between successive heart beats as the heart fills with blood (cf. systole).

dorsal of the upper surface, or back (cf. ventral).

endoscopy the use of a fibreoptic machine to see inside certain areas of the body, typically the lungs but also, potentially, other areas such as the rectum or the uterus.

epidermalization the regrowth of skin at the edge of a wound.

eversion the turning inside out of something such as an organ, for example the bladder or the uterus.

excoriation damage done by abrasion, such as scratching an inflamed area.

extension the straightening out of an area, or of a joint (cf. flexion).

faradism use of an electrical current applied to the skin to stimulate the underlying muscles and nerves.

fistula an unnatural, narrow opening.

flexion the bending of an area, such as a joint (cf. extension).

foreign body any item that does not naturally exist in or on the body, such as a thorn in the skin, or dirt in a wound.

granulation tissue the tissue that fills in the base of a wound that is left open; it is of granular appearance (hence the name), bright pink, and has little sensation, but it bleeds easily.

hernia the protrusion of tissue from within the body through an enlarged opening in the body wall. It often lies beneath the skin as a swelling (cf. rupture).

hyoid apparatus the bony structures that support the larynx within the throat and allow swallowing to occur.

hyperthermia overheating of the body; a body temperature that is above normal.

hypothermia excessive cooling of the body; body temperature that is below normal.

ingestion the oral taking in of matter.

inhalation the breathing in of matter.

lameness limping; unsoundness of limb.

lavage washing out (e.g. of a wound).

longitudinal of length; running lengthwise (cf. transverse).

manipulation the moving of matter, such as a muscle or joint, with the hands.

medulla the inner part of many organs and bone; within the cortex.

neurological of the nervous system.

open fracture fracture associated with a skin wound, and hence susceptible to outside contamination.

palpation physically feeling or sensing with the hands.

peritonitis inflammation of the lining of the abdomen (the peritoneum).

photosensitization the process of becoming sensitive to light.

pleuritis inflammation of the lining of the chest or thorax (the pleurae).

prehend to take into the mouth.

prolapse the slipping down or moving out of an organ, so that is comes to lie outside of the structures in which it is normally situated.

pthisis bulbi shrivelling of the eyeball, usually following an injury.

recumbency lying down; inability or unwillingness to stand.

rostral of the side nearest the head of the horse.

rupture the protrusion of an internal organ or tissue through an abnormal opening in the body wall; generally caused by an injury.

sedation the process of making a horse less aware of its surroundings, and thus less sensible of stress or pain, by administering a drug designed for the purpose.

septicaemia the entry of infection to the bloodstream.

sequelae the results (e.g. the effects of a disease or injury).

synovial of joints and bursae, i.e. those structures that contain joint fluid.

systole the beat of the heart, involving muscular contraction of the walls of the heart (cf. diastote).

tendinitis inflammatory disease of the tendon.

toxaemia the entry of toxins into the bloodstream.

tranquillization the process of making a horse calmer, or otherwise reducing his level of consciousness, by administering a drug designed for the purpose.

transverse arranged or running crosswise; in cross-section (cf. longitudinal).

tuber coxa the bony protuberance of the pelvis associated with the point of the hip.

tuber ischii the bony protuberances of the pelvis on either side of the tail base.

tuber sacrale the bony protuberances of the pelvis associated with its connection to the spine.

unilateral of one side (cf. bilateral and contralateral).

ventral of the underside (cf. dorsal).

Further Reading ———

Bromiley, Mary, *Equine Injury and Therapy*, Blackwell Scientific (1987).

Hayes, Horace, *Veterinary Notes for Horse Owners*, Stanley Paul (1989).

Hickman, John, and Humphreys, Martin, *Hickman's Farriery*, J. A. Allen (1988).

Index